Musical Instruments

Lucie Rault

Musical
Instruments

Craftsmanship and Traditions from Prehistory to the Present

Harry N. Abrams, Inc., Publishers

116706

To my parents
Anahide Davidian and Jean Rault

and to my children
Pierre-Iskander, Lionel Armen and Lore-Anaïs Leyrat

Translated from the French *Instruments de musique du monde*
by Jane Brenton

Library of Congress Card Number: 00-106603

ISBN 0-8109-4384-0

Printed and bound in Italy

Harry N. Abrams, Inc.
100 Fifth Avenue
New York, N.Y. 10011
www.abramsbooks.com

116706

Contents

The Chinese *erhu* fiddle, an essential member of both classical and popular ensembles (see p. 157).

The *sarangi* fiddle of India, played by a street musician in Jodhpur (see p. 90).

Samburu women in Kenya performing ritual ululation, using their hands to modulate the continuous wailing sound (see pp. 56–7).

Whirling Dervishes in Egypt performing their traditional stately gyrations to musical accompaniment (see p. 64).

Introduction

This book does not claim to be a comprehensive survey of the instruments of the world. In attempting to rethink the relationship of man and music, and examining the early motivations of his search for sound, it adopts an approach more intuitive than scholarly, more instinctive than methodical. Any attempt to explain the background to musical instruments involves a process of tracing back to their source all the relevant phenomena, gestures and impulses, in the hope of discovering a fundamental approach common to all musical activity, wherever the presence of man has been detected.

Creating musical instruments involves a respect for the materials sublimated in their construction, it means discovering and appreciating their acoustic and magical qualities. In this sphere perhaps more than any other, man has shown himself to be tireless and patient, proceeding methodically and in harmony with his environment, coming to terms with local factors – relief, climate, vegetation, animal species.

In so far as one can pin down the origins, sound was the means by which the early hominids first judged distance, whether by use of the voice or by other means, taking advantage of the phenomena of echoes and resonance. This awareness of the carrying power of the voice, and of its modulation by the immediate environment, was subsequently crucial in the choice of suitable materials and forms. No doubt the imitation of natural sounds and animal calls constituted man's very first 'musical' repertoire, reflecting his desire to influence the natural order. His relationship with animals, and their role as protective agents through the medium of magic and dance, has remained virtually unchanged over the centuries, at least within social groups whose cultures continue to treat nature and animals with respect, in a reciprocal relationship rather than one of sterile domination.

Primitive instruments were also available as found objects, either in their natural state or shaped by natural external phenomena: hollow quill feathers, whistles made of animal phalanxes, conch shells, stalactites forming stone organs etc. The progressive improvement of these 'natural' instruments was combined with a heavy injection of symbolic content, referring to a social structure or to cultural and religious allegiances.

The music played in those distant times did not reflect a desire to create melody, far from it. There was no 'artistic' approach, in the modern sense of sound effects and impressions being designed to form part of a musical composition. The common understanding today is that instruments are for 'making music', but how often are the stages of their development and history ignored. Before they came to be used in entertainments, many instruments were more or less ritual objects having an acoustic function, subsuming within themselves not only timbre and rhythm but a wide range of meanings made explicit in their form, materials and voice.

The creation of devices capable of producing resonance was the culmination of a long and patient exploration of sounds. Contrasting and complementary timbres were created first with the voice, when harmonics were produced within the oral cavity, then through the selection of suitable lengths of flexible reed or string. The player's fingers were used to explore intervals, set up repetitions, span octaves. Once the use of strings became diversified, musical thinking became more complex, or at least a different kind of thinking took over; another voice, sublimated in the music, was revealed – a voice from the soul, addressed to the soul.

Once an instrument had been conceived of – a sort of double of the self, as well as a composite object developed in accordance with a tradition – a rapid evolution followed comparing and contrasting, perfecting and diversifying, its momentum the more unstoppable because the instrument is the means of translating thought itself into something visible, palpable and audible. Only then was it possible for man to have a true dialogue with this interlocutor, this triumph of his ingenuity.

Opposite: *The courtesan Harogi, under the spell of mysterious sounds* (detail). From the set of prints *Snow, moon and flowers* by Kitagawa Utamaro (1753–1806).

1   The Voices of Nature

In the beginning there was sound

The repertory of sounds occurring in nature has had a fundamental influence on human development, not least by instilling in people's minds certain impressions and sensations. Waterfalls, the surge of the tide, the whistling of the wind, thunder, the crackle of fire … all these auditory experiences, often accompanied by visual manifestations, appeared to be voices coming from elsewhere. Because they defied explanation, they were assumed to emanate from spirits or divinities. It is this gamut of natural sounds that has formed the basis of the primary aural palette familiar to man from prehistoric times to the present day. Logical and rational explanations of these phenomena have been available to man ever since the development of scientific knowledge, yet such primordial sounds still have the power to impress us today.

The divine echo

The echo effect is probably the most fundamental sound experience known to man since the earliest times. From this first physical experiment, of giving voice and eliciting a response, derives the whole range of exploration of the phenomena of natural resonance, initially within one's own body, and then through other bodies in the immediate environment, whether in the open or in enclosed spaces.

That early quasi-musical phenomenon was accompanied by the first stirrings of human spirituality. There being no scientific explanation available to account for the 'response' elicited, the echo was seen as arising from some unknown and unpredictable realm of nature beyond the human compass. It seems likely therefore that the spiritual impulse common to all human beings has its origins in, and develops from, the emission of sounds. The echo of one's own voice was interpreted as a divine response, and this gave rise to

the construction of a belief system that incorporates elements present in nature – mountains, valleys, rocks, trees and plants, wind and clouds, thunder and lightning: in fact everything that reflects the echo and, by the same token, everything that gives tongue or produces sound.

Anything perceived by the eye is brought to life by the sound it emits, and in this fashion all the elements of creation have life breathed into them and acquire the power to communicate with mankind. Human beings appear to have been endowed from the first with a creative faculty which was exploited in order to discover a superior being and persuade that being to respond; in this manner, man communicates with another dimension.

It is clear then that the realm of sound was intimately linked with man's desire to isolate and construct, to the best of his ability, a system of belief. More than any others, so-called primitive peoples are receptive to nature and model their life and attitudes upon it. In that respect their sensibility has nothing in common with so-called developed peoples who have lost their receptiveness to any way of thinking not based on reason. This mode of thought, characteristic of what the influential anthropologist Claude Lévi-Strauss dubbed the 'savage mind', proceeds tentatively, by trial and error, and it allows primitive people to relate to those natural phenomena that are capable of immediate apprehension without trapping them in a scientific construct that will inevitably lead to a desire for domination and appropriation. Such a coherent approach implies a profound respect for natural phenomena, as well as an attitude not automatically governed by fear or submission: the dominant motive is rather a desire for harmony, with human beings seen as occupying their due place within the natural order, and maintaining to the best of their ability an equilibrium between the forces of heaven and earth.

Preceding double page: A storm on the African plains (Kenya). Sudden discharges of energy create a spectacular display in the sky and send peals of thunder crashing around the landscape.

Right: Skógafoss waterfall in Iceland. An example of a natural phenomenon that offers an auditory experience to match its imposing visual beauty.

The music of caves

From the start prehistoric man must have been struck by the phenomenon of the echo in the caves he inhabited. In these places of absolute silence and total darkness, disturbed only by the sound of dripping water magnified out of all proportion, imagine the effect of the human or animal voice amplified by what was in effect a resonating chamber of stone. For these grottoes function as immense echo chambers, and their natural vaults are capable of producing an acoustic not dissimilar to what one might hear in some Romanesque chapel. Cave dwellers lived in environments that were perfect mechanisms for projecting sounds, and it is legitimate therefore to regard such environments as the first musical instruments available to man, even though they were formed by nature long before any experimentation with instruments of his own devising was attempted.

Recent acoustic experiments carried out in caves under the direction of Iégor Reznikoff have shown that in the majority of cases the presence of wall paintings and drawings is linked to the phenomenon of the natural echo. Furthermore it has been established that indications relating to sound are recorded, not in the form of random graffiti

dispersed at the whim of the artist, but as precisely coded signs within the pictorial representation, thus indicating, often by means of lines or dots emerging from the mouth of a person or animal, those areas where the echo is at its most pronounced. Such a correlation between sound and sign can be traced back to the age of Neanderthal Man.

Three caves in the Ariège region of France – Niaux, Le Fontanet and Le Portel – were investigated and subjected, just as though they were musical instruments, to an examination of their acoustic properties. The experiments were concerned principally with the length and intensity of sounds, and more generally with the way resonances varied in relation to the point of emission.

The sound data for Le Fontanet showed no significant variations – perhaps because the original entrance had been blocked by subsequent post-glacial rock deposits, effectively transforming an 'open pipe' into a 'closed' one. But both Le Portel, which has three entirely separate galleries, and Niaux, which is an exceptionally large cave system, provide clear sets of results. The configuration of these caverns, give or take a few adjustments, has remained unchanged since the Palaeolithic Age, apart from some variations that may have occurred in the thickness of the walls or in the

Above: Entrance to the Grotte du Pech-Merle (Lot). The red dots on the roof of the cave indicate a zone of particular acoustic significance.

Double page overleaf:
The constant flow of water filtering through the mass of rock has eaten away a passage which, seen in relief, resembles the form of the cochlea, the spiral cavity of the inner ear. Antelope Canyon, Arizona.

Acoustic phenomena

The convoluted inner passage of the human ear twists and turns rather in the manner of a winding cavern. It is almost like a rocky cave in microcosm: both ear and cave perform the function of receptors, funnelling sound and setting up resonances like an organ pipe.

The fundamental purpose of the ear is to pick up sound waves within a certain spectrum and communicate them to the brain, which then identifies their frequency from the impulses transmitted to the auditory nerve.

The number of vibrations, or cycles, per second that can be registered by the human ear is calculated in hertz (Hz), while the magnitude of these vibrations is expressed in decibels (dB). The pitch of a sound depends on the number of vibrations per second, which may also be called the frequency. A lower number of vibrations per second produces a deeper sound, while a greater number of vibrations results in a higher pitch. The power and amplitude of the vibrations will determine their intensity, which in turn, when experienced subjectively, will depend on pitch and timbre. The latter is a function of the numbers, pitch and modalities of association of the harmonics that are present. Each sound source produces a fundamental or natural tone as it vibrates, and this is accompanied by other weaker and higher-pitched tones called harmonics, whose frequency is always a multiple of the fundamental frequency. A very short sound is sometimes hard for the ear to register, and therefore if a sound is heard clearly it is presumed to be of sufficient duration.

The human ear has a range of hearing with an upper limit corresponding to the threshold of pain, while its lower limit, corresponding to the threshold of hearing, marks the level below which sounds remain imperceptible. The areas above and below the normal range of human hearing are the acoustic domains respectively of ultrasonics and infrasonics.

Different natural objects can produce sounds of the same pitch and the same intensity, but the timbre may be quite distinct because of differences in the materials and their mode of vibration. Timbre is particularly significant where primordial sounds are concerned, as these are perceived as voices expressing themselves through a material reality and identified therefore, like any voice, by individual characteristics.

Solid bodies – flat or curved plaques, hollow objects, boards and tubes – as well as flexible bodies – blades, strings or membranes – are all capable of producing sound, whether this is achieved by percussion, rubbing, plucking or blowing. Man has traditionally drawn his materials from the natural environment – animal, vegetable and mineral – and used them in association with the four elements: fire, air, earth and water.

Side-blown conch shell from the Marquesas Islands. The deep, muted quality of the sound is attributable in part to the spiral form of the shell's interior. L. 38 cm (15 in.).

Palaeolithic wall paintings of
a stag's head (left) and a bison
(right), in the Black Salon of
the Grotte de Niaux, Ariège.
The paintings are positioned
to correspond with those
spots capable of producing
prolonged echoes of a
particular intensity.

ground-level due to the laying down of sediments; such changes would have the effect of modifying the pitch of sounds but not the intervals between frequencies. We can therefore safely assume that the resonance of the caves as they exist today is substantially the same as it was when they were inhabited and when the walls were decorated.

The acoustic studies were carried out using the human voice, keeping within the restricted range of a fifth without any need for amplification. There was minimal vibration therefore, both in respect of the sound emitted from the body and of that subsequently magnified by the resonance specific to the grotto, which produced harmonics proportionate to the original sound frequencies. The

parallel between the vibration of the body and that of the grotto is crucial, because man is central to this experiment, in which he uses the cave as his echo chamber. Depending on its configuration, the interior dictates a restricted range of vocal emissions, so that the resonance in the human body may occur for example at the level of the cranium or of the chest. Sometimes the effect is to make the singer emit a sound little louder than a whisper, with only the echo of the harmonic fifth to indicate the fundamental or natural note.

Once some sort of echo map had been drawn up with the aid of markers on the wall, it became clear that the modifications of the sound corresponded to a pattern of acoustic nodes and antinodes specific to a particular

The echoing grotto

The echo map isolates a number of locations favourable for the emission or the reflection of sound. Other spots are characterized by their ability to modify or amplify sound, even to the point of acoustical saturation. And finally there are zones that generate or prolong sounds for precise lengths of time. These are described as harmonic vectors. When all these sound-sensitive points that have been identified are plotted on an acoustical map, the result provides a very close correlation with a map based on the pictorial data.

Most of the locations favourable for the emission of sound correspond more or less exactly to a painted image on the wall. In locations that are exceptionally favourable, such as the 'camarin' recess in the Breuil Gallery at Le Portel, the least whisper reverberates in such a way that one is induced to make low-pitched mooing sounds, which echo throughout the gallery in impressive fashion. Moreover, the decoration of this recess is as exceptional as the sounds that emanate from it, for most of the animal species featured in the cave are grouped together in this spot. Equally, there are many recesses in other parts of the Breuil Gallery that are characterized by having neither echo, figure nor sign.

Another particularly favourable location is at the far end of the Régnault Gallery. From this point, the echo is reflected back along the whole length of the gallery (the walls of which are covered with horses), as well as a good hundred yards into the next chamber, the walls of which are similarly lined with images.

There is a question that must inevitably be asked. Were the walls chosen because of the acoustic properties they possessed, so that sound could be used to enhance the image, or was the sound itself regarded as sufficiently important actually to inspire a particular image? Although the two hypotheses are not mutually exclusive, the situation remains far from clear. Yet there are places where marks on the wall can only correspond to sound data, and in such cases it has been possible to submit the acoustic points marked on the wall to a sound test. The experiment was carried out in total darkness, with only the sound serving as a guide in determining where the sound-sensitive areas ought to be located – and where indeed they eventually proved to be, often identified only by a red dot in places where a larger figure could not have been accommodated.

A detailed plan of the Le Portel cave has been established, giving the precise locations of the sound-sensitive spots and the marks, dots and signs that correspond to them, together with comprehensive specifications for the four galleries, Jeannel, Jammes, Régnault and Breuil. Among the animals represented in the Jeannel Gallery, we note the presence of an owl at the exit from a straight passage with the keynote A, where the dominant image is that of a bison; next a G, which is indicated by short straight lines and splashes of black; then another A, marked by the owl, followed by a G with the representation of a horse; and finally an A accompanied by an ox. Thus, the sequence of drawings follows the sound oscillation A,G,A,G,A.

configuration. As in the case of any musical instrument, the actual form of each grotto directly influenced its individual acoustic properties. Several factors are relevant here. First, the 'keynote' of the 'pipe', or in other words the fundamental note specific to certain galleries. Effectively, each grotto is in a certain key: for some it may be D, for others A, or it may be in several keys. A second factor is a complex set of resonances displaying quite considerable variations (ranging from five to six seconds in certain locations to something of much shorter duration in others), depending on whether the resonance exhibits dramatic oscillations or remains flat. This is not in fact an echo, but sound amplified either in intensity or length.

The enigma of the horned hunter and his bow

Grotte des Trois Frères, Montesquieu-Avantès (Ariège).

Simplified detail of a Magdalenian wall painting discovered and copied in 1912 by Abbé Breuil.

The lower section of wall in the Sanctuary of Les Trois Frères bears the engraving of a human figure with the skin of a bison, horns and tail included, pulled over his head and back and partially covering them. He is in pursuit of the deer which are shown.

We would no doubt be right to link this scene with representations of other dancing figures wearing animal skins that have been discovered at various sites in southern France. Although there is considerable disagreement over the nature of the instrument depicted in two lines, one straight, the other curving, it would seem most to resemble a musical bow (as originally identified by Abbé Breuil). The leg movements suggest that the figure is performing a dance, while at the same time vibrating the string of his bow, the end of which he holds in his mouth, in accordance with the technique traditionally adopted for playing the mouth-held bow.

Probably what is recorded here is a scene of the hunter approaching his quarry in a practice that remains current even today among certain Asiatic and Amerindian populations, who see the animal they hunt as their totem and ancestor. Running with the herd, they perform a magic dance in which the man becomes one with the animal he is pursuing, not only in terms of appearance, but also in respect of it cries which he mimics with the aid of an animal-lure: this ritual communion with the intended victim provides the justification for the hunt, which thus becomes a sacrificial act.

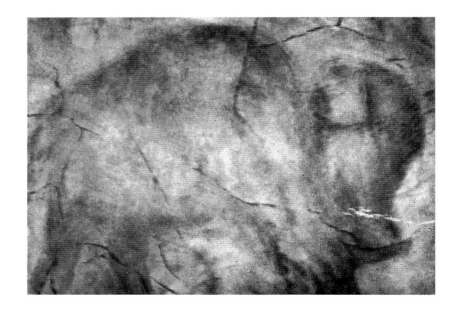

Left to right: Horse, in the gallery of the Black Salon of the Grotte de Niaux, Ariège; mammoth painted on the wall of the Kapovaya cave, Bashkir (Southern Urals); horse and bison, Grotte du Portel, Ariège. The representation of each type of figure may well be associated with a characteristic echo.

In the Jammes Gallery, at the entrance to the Gallery of the Horses, the appearance of an echo in A (which is a fifth above the fundamental note for this gallery) is marked on the left by a splash of red and on the right by the image of a small horse, also in red. Corresponding to the transition to G, as one progresses down towards the end of the gallery, is a panel representing a horse, a goat-like creature and some deer. Next, one comes to a crucial sound node, which is situated in a central resonance space, within sight of a large red sign, an anamorphosed horse and an ithyphallic figure. Splashes of red and a variety of other figures decorate the back of the gallery, where the dominant echo is the D of the octave above; this echo extends for approximately 115 metres (125 yards), right into the Jeannel Gallery, where it terminates abruptly in front of the image of the owl. The places that reflect the echoes are precisely those where the paintings are concentrated: harmonic intervals of a fifth are associated with the various sound-sensitive points and their accompanying wall paintings. The exception is a third, an F sharp, that corresponds to a recess containing a representation of a fish, a creature that features only rarely in rock art.

The research study has also revealed the existence of sound 'doorways', like the one marked by the owl, a bird known to possess exceptionally acute hearing. These doorways lead into spaces filled with images. It would probably be appropriate therefore to read some symbolic significance into the representations of the different animals and their relationship to the particular echoes measured in their vicinity.

As far as the Régnault Gallery is concerned, there are no echoes until the first alcove is reached, which is precisely the point where the first images appear: headless animals, coinciding with the emergence of the keynote E; a deer, also headless, corresponding to the appearance of an F; then a bison falling and the head of an ox, coinciding with the appearance of a B. Further on, a narrow bottleneck produces prolonged echoes in D: here the red dot visible on the roof

can only be a sound-sensitive sign. As the gallery narrows towards the end, the representations on the walls are paralleled by a further pattern of resonances in which D and G figure largely; these two notes are perpetuated with particular force right into the Jammes Gallery, most especially in the region of the ithyphallic figure. It is in those places where the echo is strongest that the presence of anthropomorphic figures is most notable.

Comparable investigations at Niaux have similarly demonstrated that in this cave places with particularly strong echoes also have images associated with them; some of these, significantly, mark places where sounds linger for several seconds. We can therefore conclude that the choice of locations for wall figures seems to have been made largely on the basis of their acoustical value. Sometimes whole walls remain empty where the corresponding space, however vast it may be, produces no echo. On the other hand, places favourable for echoes are marked and painted, even if their location made such decoration difficult to accomplish.

Prehistoric man must have experienced caves as living organisms, especially if he explored their interior spaces in semi-darkness. He must have apprehended their supernatural dimension initially through the awesome reverberations that sounded throughout the cavern – sensations which he subsequently reinforced by means of images. These two-dimensional images then became evocations of the entities represented and became elements in a magical process.

The voice and its double

There can be little doubt that in Palaeolithic times people used their voices to experiment with these phenomena of resonance, given that vocal vibrations especially in the lower registers, lasted longer than any other type of sound. The basic primitive vocalization consisted in the emission of the vowels a and o, or in humming the sounds 'mm' or 'hm'

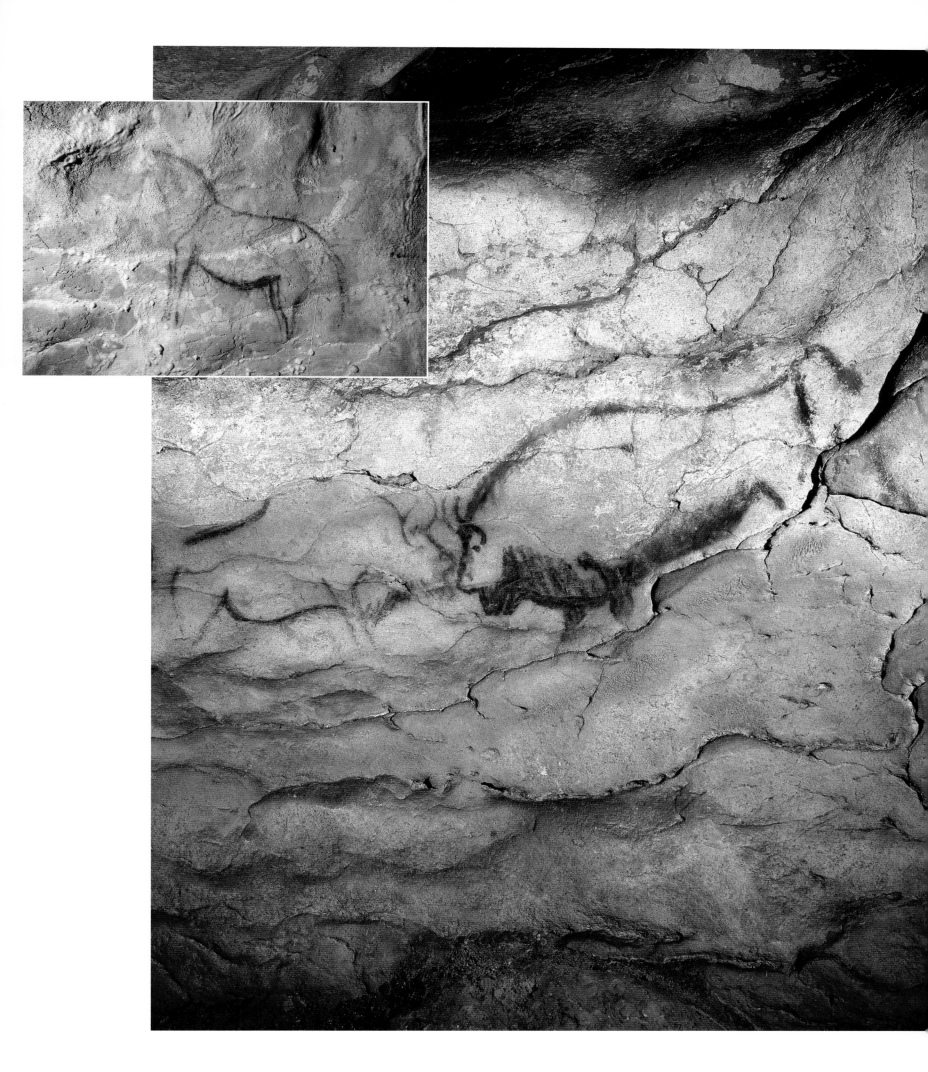

while keeping the mouth shut: prehistoric man must have arrived at this method instinctively, particularly in view of the fact that he occupied such a favourable acoustic environment where even the slightest, most tentative sound was intensified or prolonged. The intervals of the unison, the fourth and the fifth – D/G or D/A – would have been used for simple melodies based on a restricted chromatic range. With the benefit of resonance and added harmonics, these sounds acquired a greater fullness and a particular colour dependent on the configuration of the place. The reverberating sound also served as a guide for the voice as man attempted to reproduce the same effect, thus expanding the original chromatic range.

Voices in a low register created a deeper and more impressive echo, and this provided the model for the sound of the earliest instruments. The preference was for something resembling either a low-pitched voice or the sound of a voice echoing inside a cavern. In both these cases therefore we encounter the phenomenon of vocal doubling, first in respect of the human voice reflected back from its surroundings, and, later, that same effect reproduced by an instrument specially created as a means of capturing this 'other' voice and controlling it. Having acquired, mastered and exploited the principle of resonance, primitive man could proceed to adapt this physical law to other material objects.

The phenomenon of doubling, consisting of call and response, implies the existence of an outside view of man and the human condition, and by extension therefore a spiritual dimension. As he groped his way along the dark passages of the caverns, prehistoric man was not only exploring sound in terms of acoustic effects but also in respect of the vibrations it created in his body and, through the physical body, his state of mind.

Strengthened by his ability to understand the phenomenon of sound, early man became conscious of the creative power inherent in it. When he created pictorial reproductions of the animals that were familiar to him in his immediate environment, he also endowed them with a voice, making them alive and tangible. And by giving the animals life he brought them within his grasp and under his control. Conscious by now that everything that vibrated, or that he caused to vibrate, was endowed with life, he set about exploiting or creating vibrating objects, as well as places in which the human voice would vibrate to best advantage. In doing this, he communicated directly with a supernatural dimension, either external or one that he sensed within himself.

Organs of stone

Among the archaeological evidence discovered in the course of investigations into acoustic phenomena in prehistoric times are fragments of material such as stone, bones and seashells – skin and vegetable materials would of course not be expected to survive. These remains, which were discovered in caves decorated with animals and other signs, allow us to make a modest attempt at recreating the inventory of prehistoric instruments, in the sense of objects

Stalactite curtain in a cave in South Africa. The cavern itself forms a natural echo chamber that amplifies and prolongs the sounds emitted by these vast natural lithophones.

that show signs of manipulation for the purpose of producing sounds. Just as certain caves possess acoustical properties that make them function as natural echo chambers, so there are certain mineral structures, notably 'organs' composed of stalactites and stalagmites, and calcite curtains, that form natural idiophones when struck and so caused to vibrate.

Several archaeological sites, among them the Régnault Gallery at Le Portel, show more or less regular alignments of stalagmite stumps, these being the result of breaks dating from the Cro-Magnon era. Since such stumps are a

frequently observed phenomenon, we may incline to the view that they were the result of a common ritual act, intentioned to produce a deafening noise like a thunder-clap. In several cases it clearly proved impossible to shatter the stone columns, which still bear a pattern of crazing caused by blows.

Some rocks formed out of curtain-like accretions of calcite can serve as natural lithophones, or stone instruments, and these produce a particularly strong sound within the space of the cavern. The vibrations they produce have been subjected to detailed study involving an evaluation of the basic frequencies emitted following percussion, and it has been possible to establish that the most effective curtains, in terms of the sound they produce, often show signs of having been gashed and broken at the points of most favourable impact. Having once discovered these various points of impact, early man would have been able to use them in a temporal and spatial sequence to create melodies of an instinctively rhythmic nature. Although not all these lithophones show physical traces of percussion, there is always evidence of wall paintings present in the vicinity.

Double page overleaf: Ladakh, in the high plains of the Himalayas. The mountain chain in the background forms a natural wall that refelcts sound waves in the form of an echo. To ensure a continuous sound, *dung-dkar* conches are always played in pairs. The musicians alternate with one another, playing the same music but pausing for breath at different times.

Below: Conch player in Zanzibar (Tanzania). This shell produces such a powerful sound that it is sometimes used in times of war as an instrument of summons to assemble the combatants.

Natural modulations

The aural background against which prehistoric man evolved was made up of an infinite variety of natural sounds that played on his emotions and helped him develop his acoustical abilities to encompass broad tonal registers, ranging from total silence to intolerably high frequencies. To recreate this world of sound, it would be necessary to imagine the cries of all the species alive in the Middle Palaeolithic (100,000–60,000 BC), the so-called Mousterian era, as well as the way of life of the human species of the time, *Homo sapiens* and *Homo neanderthalensis*, and exactly the same for the Upper Palaeolithic (40,000–10,000 BC), which is subdivided into the Aurignacian, the Gravettian, the Solutrean and the Magdalenian, during which *Homo sapiens* was the sole human species. The sounds associated with the various animal species were extensively exploited by man in those distant times, particularly in the use of imitation, to allow him to approach closer to game. The vast repertoire of cries and calls used among the animals themselves – alarms, threats, mating calls etc. – the various whistles and songs of birds, the buzzing and humming of insects, in addition to all the noises in the natural environment, such as thunder, rain, the rustling of leaves in the wind, combined

to form the backdrop of sounds against which man would, in time, intervene to leave his own musical imprint, marking his place in space or in silence.

It was through the sounds he emitted that man discovered his identity, as one species among many, one social group among others, and one individual within a community. Particular sound frequencies were conditioned by the natural vegetation and relief, and certain of these gained currency because they were particularly well adapted to a specific environment: thus a mountainous relief favoured high-pitched sounds that carry over long distances from one summit to the next. This encouraged the natural impulse to whistle, and led in turn to the use of instrumental whistles emitting high-frequency sound.

Animals and the power of sound

Among the most ancient musical instruments of which traces were found in caves dating from the Aurignacian era, the whistle made from the phalanx of a reindeer represents a decisive step in the manufacture of musical instruments. Such phalanxes are naturally hollow, as indeed are the first and second phalanxes of members of the species cervidae (deer) and ovidae (sheep), and these particular examples are marked by traces of animal bites; the playing holes must have been either enlarged from the original bite marks, or pierced in the form of the perfectly circular holes that occur in other positions. Researches have shown that these bite marks were inflicted by the reindeer's natural predator, the wolf. The use of the human hand to transform these phalanxes into whistles implies a triangular exchange between man, wolf and reindeer, the two former being predators of the latter.

Apart from the communication possibilities offered by whistles such as these, we need to consider the effect of these whistling noises on animal behaviour. In experiments conducted on herds of reindeer using identical whistles made of reindeer phalanxes, resembling both the Palaeolithic example and the type still in regular use among the Indian peoples of north-west Canada, it was observed that the animal would stand still the moment they heard whistle being blown; then, when the call had been repeated several times at intervals of a few minutes, they would lie down and remain motionless. On the other hand the use of a 'pea' whistle, of the type employed by traffic police, had the effect of making the animals take flight after standing still and listening only briefly.

Spectrum analysis shows that the frequency of the pea whistle does not correspond to the straight line that is characteristic of the sound produced by a bone whistle, but appears as a shallow wavy line of the type that corresponds to a low and repeated frequency, reflecting the movement of the ball inside the whistle. The unstable quality of the sound is perceived by the animals as a significant threat and causes them to take flight.

These experiments demonstrate not only the effects that sounds can produce in animal behaviour, but also the fact that the animals can distinguish the type of instrument

Double page overleaf: The side-blown *embe* horn made of the spiral horn of a member of the deer family (Rwanda), and the conch-shape trumpet *dung-dkar* played by a young Buddhist monk (Tibet). An animal horn or shell can be made into a musical instrument with a rich and powerful sound simply by piercing it with an approximately round hole.

being used and the nature of the whistle emitted. A short blast may be enough to stop an animal in its tracks, though it remains wary and on the defensive (as is the case with bears and even hares, which rear up and remain frozen to the spot, allowing the hunter to get closer to his prey), while a long, repeated whistle deprives it of any defensive instinct. This is particularly true of members of the deer family, who are known to be sensitive to the soothing power of sounds: certain frequencies have a direct effect on the animal's nervous system.

The mechanical animal-calls used by hunters are made of specific materials, either derived from the creature being hunted or representing it in some symbolic fashion. A form of magic is involved that has to do with the relationship that exists between the different species. In this connection the power of sound, relayed through the intermediary of the animal-call or musical instrument, plays a universally recognized role.

It is of course possible for man to imitate the sounds of birds and animals by using the mouth, with or without the aid of fingers. However, the introduction of a symbolic element taken from the natural world, and if possible from the body of an animal of the species being summoned, lends the act a magical significance, establishing and emphasizing a tangible link between nature, animal and man. In the case of the whistle fashioned from a reindeer phalanx, another agency comes into play in this multiple relationship, namely the predatory wolf which has left its distinctive mark in the form of scratches or bites on the bones of its prey.

And yet, as far as prehistoric sites are concerned, not all the phalanxes that bear the mark of animal perforations are capable of making whistling sounds, any more than all deliberately pierced phalanxes are in fact whistles. Investigations do, however, show instances where Neanderthal Man and Cro-Magnon Man transformed phalanxes already perforated by wolf bites. Where the bone is bitten, a conical groove is formed, the angle and position of which condition the sound quality. Sometimes the mark left by the animal bite has not been added to and an aperture has been made elsewhere, in order to achieve a better quality of sound. The sound is of higher frequency if the hole is made larger, and depends also on the length of the phalanx.

Notched flute, *kena*, made from an animal bone. Colombia.

Cro-Magnon whistles

Whistling sounds form part of some of the most ancient modes of communication. Rather like birds, which have an infinite variety of calls at their disposal, there are peoples who have developed whistling techniques descended from those of Cro-Magnon Man. Such 'languages' can still be heard today – among the Wayapi in Guiana, in the Caucasus, on the island of La Gomera in the Canaries, and in the Basque country. Whistling with the mouth depends on the use of various positions of the lips and of the tongue in relation to the teeth and the palate, and the fingers and hands can also be used to modify the intonation. In order to whistle, it is only necessary to cup one's hands together and cause the air emitted from the mouth to vibrate within. The form of most whistles is based on this principle: they are hollow objects, tubular, globular or spiral, against the edge of which one blows, causing the column of emitted air to vibrate. Natural whistles usually produce only one sound, which may be varied according to the angle of inclination or the intensity of the breath; if size permits, one or more holes to make a globular flute that will produce up to three distinct tones. But even with a whistle that produces one note only, it is possible – as happens in Africa and Melanesia – to create rhythms and melodies by the use of different timbres. Musical scales and instruments such as the pan-pipes and the Chinese mouth organ were based on the technique of cutting sections of bamboo into different lengths to make whistles of different pitches, and then arranging them in order of height. To judge by the large number of whistles found in archaeological excavations, and their wide distribution, it seems likely that this type of instrument was one of the first used by prehistoric man. Since the end of the nineteenth century numerous finds of phalanxes have been made in Europe, notably those belonging to members of the cervidae family – antelopes, ibex, chamois, red deer, roe deer, reindeer – and to horses. The oldest known example belongs to an ibex and dates from *c.* 60,000 BC, the era of Neanderthal Man. It has been established that such items as these were employed first and foremost as musical instruments. Tests carried out to establish their acoustical properties have revealed a sharp, piercing sound of excellent quality, which would have been an undoubted asset for a hunter.

The fact that even today the bones of winged creatures are used by some peoples as whistles tends to confirm that such bones were always used in this manner. The Arapaho Indians of Nebraska use very similar whistles made of wild turkey bones. These emit two distinct sounds, depending on which end one blows into. Traditionally they were signals used in warfare; one to announce the attack, the other the retreat. Three of the hollow bones that form the bird's wing are favoured for use as whistles such as these: the humerus, ulna and radius – the last of these being particularly suitable as an ultrasound whistle, if small enough. They are used exactly as they are, except that both ends can be blocked and a playing hole bored in the side, or one or both ends can be left open. Given the various ways in which it is possible to breathe into hollow bones or to blow down

them, one can imagine all sorts of other uses, apart from their musical function, to which they might be put.

Like some Indian tribes in North America, the Arctic-dwelling Inuit use a naturally hollow quill as a whistle. Condor and swan's feathers, in various lengths and diameters, may be used in this way. Alongside this natural instrument there exist whistles that exploit particular plant shapes, favoured as much for the quality of the sound they produce as for their anthropomorphic appearance. One example is a forked piece of wood resembling a face, with knots indicating the eyes and the two branches being horns, each having a feather inserted in it. This improvised instrument is used by blowing down the main stem, causing the two quills at the top to act as pipes, in essentially the same way as in the case of a single feather. Many other materials can be used to make whistles, ranging from naturally perforated stone to dried fruits, or reeds and bamboos cut in a variety of lengths or fitted with some sort of internal device.

Snail shells, when pierced with a more or less round hole in the manner of an ocarina, can be played by modifying the size of the aperture so as to obtain a variety of different sounds. However, certain pierced shells of the species *Nassa neritea*, found on such European sites as Les Eyzies-de-Tayac, which was inhabited by Cro-Magnon Man, or in the Grimaldi caves situated near the border of the Italian province of Liguria, are in fact constituents of jewelry, belts or hair ornaments and not musical instruments at all. Easier to play is the larger shell of *Cassis saburon*, dating from the latter part of the Magdalenian, which was discovered at La Tourasse in Haute-Garonne. This type of aerophone is still made today in Poitou, using the shell of the common garden snail (*petit-gris*).

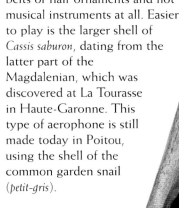

Palaeolithic flutes discovered at Isturitz (Pyrénées-Atlantiques). The fragment on the left exhibits three fingerholes and fine incisions forming regular bands. Archaeological research has permitted the reconstruction of the example on the right, featuring four fingerholes on the lower surface.

Right: Bull-roarer made of reindeer antler found at La Roche, near Lalinde in the Dordogne. Instruments of the same type are still in use today in regions of Africa and Australia. L. 17.5 cm (6¾ in.).

Opposite: Bull-roarer and its Australian aboriginal player. The sound produced by this simple plaque of wood is unlike any other acoustical phenomenon. The sight and use of bull-roarers is restricted to a small number of initiates.

The flutes of Isturitz

Pipes function in essentially the same way as whistles, by utilizing a resonating cavity (in this case the pipe itself) a bevelled edge and a jet of air blown from the user's lips. The only evidence for their use in prehistoric times are the remains of simple tubes, often in pieces. In practice, only a bone like the ulna of a large raptor could provide a pipe with a circular section sufficiently long to constitute a viable natural instrument.

At Isturitz (Pyrénées-Atlantiques) in southern France, a deposit proved to be particularly rich in flutes. Such instruments were found in the levels corresponding to the earliest Aurignacian era (30,000 BC) and the Upper Périgordian (24,000 BC), as well as the Upper Solutrean (19,000 BC). Among the finds is an almost complete flute with a bevelled mouthpiece and four fingerholes. Analysis suggests that a pentatonic scale was employed, with astonishing possibilities for creating variations in pitch. We do not know how it was played, but it may have been held at an angle, with the breath directed against the rim.

Also in a remarkable state of preservation is a flute made from the ulna of a vulture. This example, found in an ossuary cave at Veyreau (Aveyron) in the upper level of the Chalcolithic (2000 BC), has five approximately circular holes on the upper face and a square aperture. To obtain a sound, one would have had to occlude the hole on the upper face almost completely by means of a cork plug, in such a way as to cause a fine stream of air to strike the base of the square aperture. It seems at least probable that playing techniques at that period might have involved the use of a plug of this type. One of the bone flutes from Dolni Věstonice (a site in Moravia, Czech Republic) was discovered with a resin plug still in place, and from this one might reasonably infer both the technique and manufacture of flutes incorporating plugging devices.

In the case of many of the bones uncovered at the site of excavations, no prima facie case can be made for treating them as flutes because they are too rudimentary; only when they exhibit a particular form of construction, with a notch or plugging device or with fingerholes, can one confidently identify them as musical instruments.

The whirr of bull-roarers

The name bull-roarer is applied to thin pieces of solid material with a hole pierced at one end, designed to be tied to a cord and swung round above the head. An example made of bone found at L'Abri du Bois de la Garenne at Saint-Marcel (Indre), which dates from the Magdalenian period. It is some 6 cm (2⅜ inches) long, indented along the sides and decorated with three circles, each having a dot in the centre (quite possibly symbolizing the turning motion described by the object). Another bull-roarer dating from the Magdalenian period, discovered at Laugerie-Basse in the Dordogne, consists of a bone 10.5 cm (4⅛ inches) in length. Both in material and form, this example resembles the prototype dating from the Mesolithic and is 11 cm (4⅜ inches) long, from Kongemosen (a late settlement in

Instruments in prehistoric times

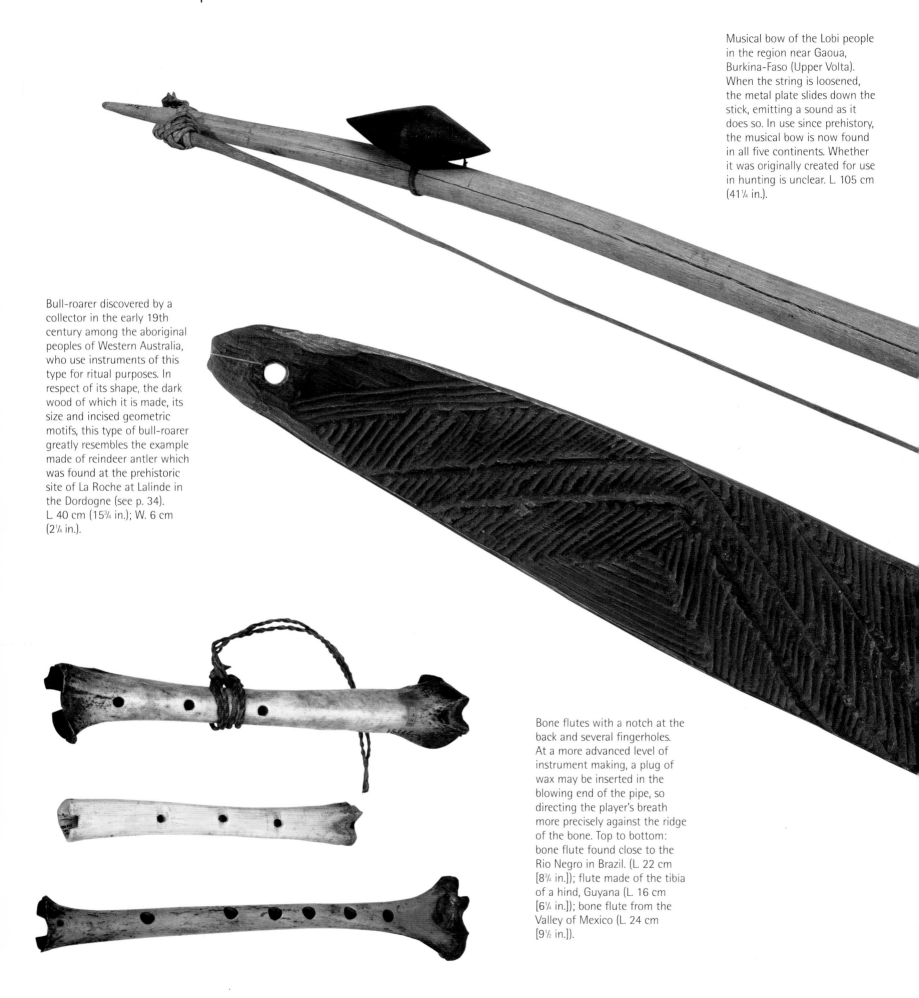

Musical bow of the Lobi people in the region near Gaoua, Burkina-Faso (Upper Volta). When the string is loosened, the metal plate slides down the stick, emitting a sound as it does so. In use since prehistory, the musical bow is now found in all five continents. Whether it was originally created for use in hunting is unclear. L. 105 cm (41¼ in.).

Bull-roarer discovered by a collector in the early 19th century among the aboriginal peoples of Western Australia, who use instruments of this type for ritual purposes. In respect of its shape, the dark wood of which it is made, its size and incised geometric motifs, this type of bull-roarer greatly resembles the example made of reindeer antler which was found at the prehistoric site of La Roche at Lalinde in the Dordogne (see p. 34). L. 40 cm (15¾ in.); W. 6 cm (2¼ in.).

Bone flutes with a notch at the back and several fingerholes. At a more advanced level of instrument making, a plug of wax may be inserted in the blowing end of the pipe, so directing the player's breath more precisely against the ridge of the bone. Top to bottom: bone flute found close to the Rio Negro in Brazil. (L. 22 cm [8¾ in.]); flute made of the tibia of a hind, Guyana (L. 16 cm [6¼ in.]); bone flute from the Valley of Mexico (L. 24 cm [9½ in.]).

Bull-roarer discovered on the island of Bougainville, Solomon Islands. In this Melanesian example the representation of the male figure is linked to the instrument's function, as it plays a part in boys' initiation rites. Although the bull-roarer is more usually associated with the Oceanic civilizations, it has a wide area of distribution and is found in Africa, North America and even in Europe (in Poland, for example). L. 79 cm (31 in.); W. 15 cm (6 in.).

Below: The scraper called *chicahuatli*, made of a section of human femur, which was discovered in a valley in Mexico (14th–16th century). This instrument was played by the Aztecs in ceremonies associated with agrarian rituals. L. 18 cm (7 in.).

Denmark). Bull-roarers dating from the Upper Magdalenian, made from the blades of reindeer antlers (for example the specimen excavated in 1930 at La Roche, near Lalinde in the Dordogne, which is 17.5 cm [6⅞ inches] in length, and engraved with a geometric pattern stained with red ochre), are of similar construction to items still in use today among the Australian aborigines. Other specimens made from mammoth ivory, dating from the Pavlovian (24,000 BC) have been found in Central Europe.

A free aerophone, the bull-roarer produces vibrations in the air around it, as it simultaneously turns on itself and is swung around in a circle. The sound produced by a particular instrument depends on its size and on the material used in its construction, and also the speed of rotation. Typically, the bull-roarer is in the shape of a fish, but it may be oval or diamond-shaped or in the form of a blade. The thinness of the material is the crucial factor in its ability to rotate. During archaeological excavations such instruments can easily be confused with other objects of similar shape such as pendants. Only by testing the object's ability to rotate and produce a hum can it be established whether the item had a musical function; this is best achieved by constructing a facsimile precisely identical in form and material, using primitive tools typical of the relevant period.

This instrument often has thin, sharp edges, although there are several known examples with notched edges. Sometimes decorative motifs are seen, as distinct from engraved geometric signs around the rim or marginal notches. Thus bull-roarers may bear quite refined images of animals (e.g. deer, bison or aurochs) or human figures, as found at Abri Morin and Le Lortet (Hautes-Pyrénées).

The cord is passed through a simple hole or through a protuberance (also pierced) at one end of the antler blade. Of course, no such cord dating from ancient times has survived, but the results of research into the nature of these cords leads us to believe that, when the object is rotated, they count for more than the precise shape of the individual bull-roarer. The way in which two strands are intertwined seems to have a direct effect on the resulting sound. If we liken this practice to that currently observable among the Inuit peoples, we may assume that in the Palaeolithic era too, and particularly in the case of bull-roarers, use was made of animal tendons stretched and twisted to form threads and cords. The humming noise produced, depending on the size and form of the bull-roarer, would

reverberate around a cave interior in particularly impressive fashion. As it happens, the deep roar produced by large antler blades bears a strange resemblance to the lowing sound made by the European bison (at a frequency of approximately 35 hertz). A further point to note is that the turning motion imparted to the blade produces a kinetic effect on the decoration, so that geometric or figurative motifs seem to spring into life, and sound appears to be accompanied by moving images.

Given that this ritual acoustic device is kept well out of sight and hidden from general view among the peoples where it is still in use today, it is more than likely that the same was true in prehistory – a view reinforced by the circumstances of discoveries made at Magdalenian sites.

Scraping a rhythm

Archaeological digs have turned up large numbers of seashells, snail shells and other molluscs, as well as teeth and fragments of pierced bone that were once worn as musical ornaments. Bone pendants dating from the Gravettian and Solutrean periods have been discovered at Isturitz. At Pekárna in Moravia, shells and deer's teeth found on the site have been reassembled to form a necklace. Bracelet rattles made of mammoth ivory were discovered at Mezin in Ukraine. A cranium covered with strings of shells, presumably a sort of rattling headdress, was excavated from an Aurignacian tomb in the Grotta delle Arene Candide in Liguria, and another, similarly decorated, at the Grotte du Cavillon, part of the Grimaldi caves near the border between the Principality of Monaco and Liguria in Italy.

Apart from such instruments resembling rattles or bells, the most common type of prehistoric idiophone was the scraper. The formal evolution of friction idiophones of the scraper type, exhibiting regular patterns of notches and raised areas, took place over a period ranging from the Mousterian to the Upper Palaeolithic. Very similar types of scraper may occur in wood, bone or stone. A number of specimens, including those discovered at the Aurignacian level at the sites of Isturitz and Pekárna, were fashioned from pierced sections of reindeer antlers. Other examples were found at levels corresponding to the Mesolithic at Çatal Hüyük in Anatolia, and at Tufting and Ostermoor in Schleswig-Holstein.

Bones with incised notches may represent the earliest known evidence of counting, as it is possible that they played a role in keeping track of time. There are numerous notched examples dating from the Magdalenian, all bearing the same number of incised marks, thirteen, which might well correspond to phases of the 28-day lunar cycle. Since these bones, when laid flat, also exhibit signs of scraping on their ridges and troughs, we may conclude that they must have been used as musical scrapers. The use of rhythmic sound to keep track of the phases of the moon implies a level of temporal awareness, and hints at the existence of a social order based on these rhythmic cycles.

It appears that scrapers are most common and most diversified during the Magdalenian era, probably because they were used for a variety of purposes. While the notches were still only tentatively inscribed at the start of the Palaeolithic, by the Solutrean they had become much more definite, and in the Magdalenian the objects used as scrapers exhibited wide variations: more refined forms came into existence, as well as composite objects like the pierced specimens mentioned above. One such scraper was discovered between the legs of the skeleton of an adolescent buried in the cave at Les Hoteaux (Ain). It bears an engraving of the forequarters of a belling stag. The top of its silhouette is suggested by the curved shape of a carnivore's bite, while on the short front part that bears the notches, below the engraving of the eyes, a round perforation represents an open mouth.

Above and opposite above: Women of the Malinke tribe in Guinea playing the *karinya* scraper, which consists of a metal tube. This type of scraper is normally played by women as part of an instrumental group consisting also of xylophones (*bala*) and bridged harps (*kora* or *bolon*), which provides the accompaniment to a repertoire of epic songs.

Woman holding a horn

Limestone relief discovered at Laussel (Dordogne) by Dr Lalanne in 1909;
Upper Aurignacian (Gravettian) and Proto-Solutrean H. 45 cm (17¾ in.).
Musée d'Aquitaine, Bordeaux

By the wall of the Grand Abri at Laussel were discovered four bas-reliefs of
female figures, the most important of which is known as *Woman holding a horn*.
This figure is carved in a block of fallen rock and bears traces of red ochre; it is
related to the Aurignacian Venus figures in respect of body proportions
(prominent belly and breasts in relation to limbs) and the frontal pose (in
contrast to the face, which is shown in profile). The woman holds what is
probably a bison horn in her right hand, in an attitude that may be interpreted
as that of a person preparing to drink. There are, however, a number of possible
explanations. It could be that this accessory relates to the symbolic association
of woman/bison. Equally, the horn may be seen as a horn of plenty and symbolic
of fertility. The presence of striations, thirteen in all, has also given rise to the
idea that this was a rhythmic instrument for marking the beat of the dance.
Scrapers are common instruments in primitive societies, made from a wide
variety of materials including bone, stone, dried fruit-husks, gourds, stalactites,
shells, tortoiseshell and bamboo. Bones with grooves dating from the
Magdalenian era may represent evidence of early attempts at recording time.
In the present instance the horn may be both a symbolic and an acoustic
instrument, used in fertility rites.

41

2   The Body as Instrument

Out of the body came forth music

A human being's first sensory experiences occur in the maternal womb, where the foetus is exposed to various sounds, which will impinge both on the body and the memory, even before consciousness has developed. Within this primordial natural cavern, against the background of the mother's heartbeat and pulsing arteries, the sound and inflections of her voice provide welcome points of reference and reassurance. The sound of the mother's voice not only has a soothing effect, but also conditions the unborn baby to be alert to sounds and rhythms in the future.

The hum of life going on all around becomes more and more clearly differentiated, and habituation brings with it the ability to recognize and identify the various aural experiences and vibrations to which the baby is exposed. The maternal womb, in which the baby is enclosed, functions as a wonderfully effective resonating chamber.

The birth of the voice

This *in utero* experience of aural phenomena is the basis of a subsequent liking for sound combinations, and it predisposes human beings to vocal expression and the invention of instruments designed to reproduce and imitate the human voice.

Immersed in a liquid environment, this person-in-the-making becomes familiar with the low, prolonged resonances characteristic of a closed aquatic world, and exposure to the air induces the new-born infant to cry out loud – the first individual act of human expression.

With this first reflex reaction to the ambient world, the baby's body, already a perfect resonator, takes over seamlessly from the maternal womb, all contact with which has abruptly ceased. The time has now come to experiment, in this new airy environment, and discover the optimum conditions for the recreation of those deep, familiar sounds and thus experience once again their frequency and beneficial effect.

As the new voice attempts to find itself and assume a reality, the primary point of reference is the mother's voice, which stands out from all others, and also the voices of people who were around her during the pregnancy. At the same time, the infant's cries and tears, laughter and babbling represent part of a gradual learning process through which an awareness of its own body and its potential is gained.

Games associated with objects that make a noise, such as rattles, ratchet rattles, musical mobiles, whistles, water whistles, percussion instruments, humming tops or xylophones, all contribute to the development of the auditory palette. In combination with games involving colours, they lay the foundations of sensual experience and language.

The new infant broadens and intensifies the search by modulating the voice and trying to push sounds to their limits. Exercising the vocal cords in this new element of freely circulating air, the child affirms a personal presence and superiority over his environment. Retaining a memory of the echoes and resonance experienced in the closed space of the womb, the infant will seek to recreate that partially or fully enclosed world in which the voice is expanded and magnified and reverberates to best effect.

A capella

From prehistoric times onwards, caves have provided the perfect solution to man's quest for a sanctuary, a sacred place appropriate to the celebration of a ritual, where words and song resound with particular intensity. Indeed,

Preceding double page: Dancing among the Bororo, one of the Fulani peoples of Niger. The tempo is set by the stamping of feet and the clapping of hands. The impressive rhythmic precision has much to do with the physical proximity of the dancers.

Opposite: Drawing by Leonardo da Vinci showing an anatomical study of a human foetus in the womb. The sounds heard *in utero* represent the unborn baby's introduction to the acoustic experiences of the outside world.

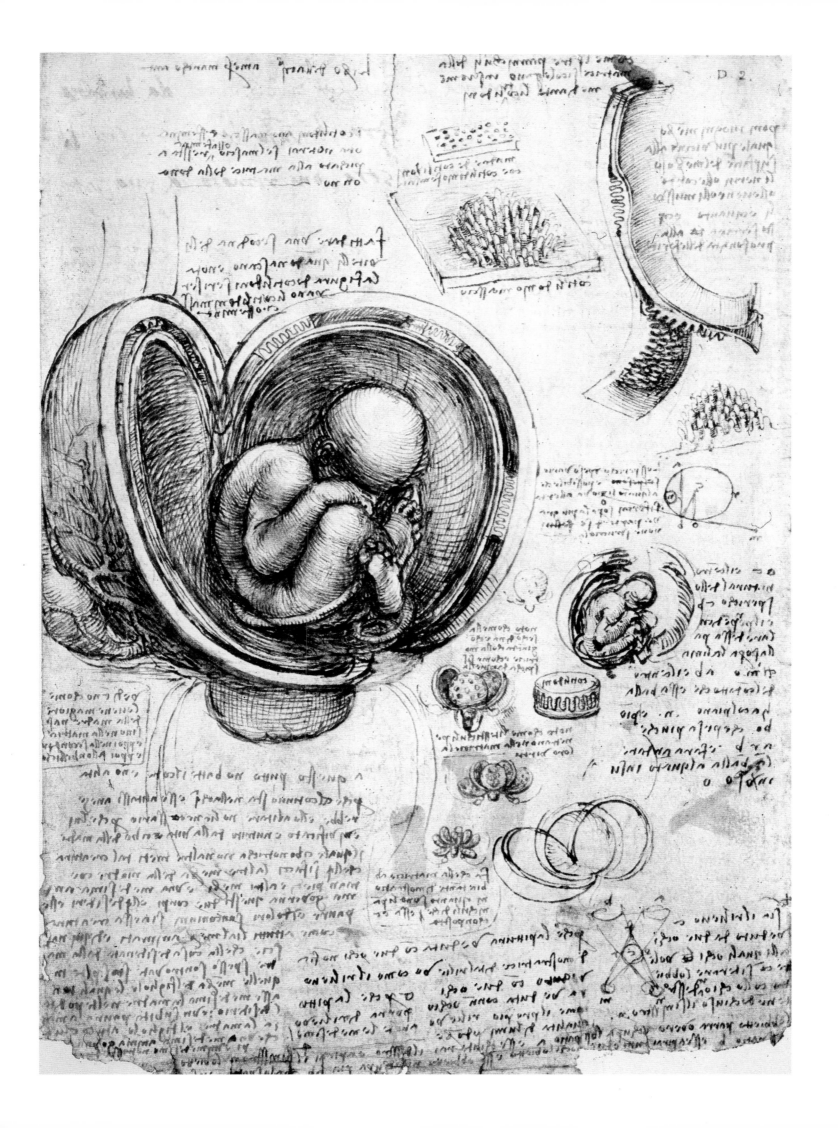

the word 'chapel' is often applied to caverns and grottoes with exceptional acoustic properties. The primary purpose of these places was to bring together a community of individuals and put them in touch with a higher dimension – which is essentially the definition of a religion.

Can it be by chance that mankind's sacred places are almost always spaces where echoes are heard to particularly good effect? Through contact with the natural world, people learned to recognize what factors were influential in helping sound to carry – for example, the presence of a natural amphitheatre surrounded by mountains, a valley or a cavity within the rock. They noticed and marked down for future reference the places that seemed to be alive, those where the voice reverberated and brought back a response in the form of an echo, where it lingered the longest or set up harmonics. They learned to control their vocal repertory, to distinguish those registers which produced the most striking sound effects, and they adapted them in order to imitate and simulate the sounds of the animals depicted in their cave paintings.

These early acoustic experiments, conducted only with the human voice, helped them to distinguish the spaces that were particularly good carriers of sound – depending on the distance the sound had to travel before encountering a physical obstacle, which might be a wall, solid rock, a low section of roof or, conversely, a rise in the roof height, where the verticals channelled the sound upward – and these experiments also aided them in reproducing similar configurations in their own constructions, even from the earliest times.

There are ancient structures famous for their exceptional acoustics, Greek and Roman theatres for example, or Celtic stone circles, or buildings like the Temple of Heaven (1530) in Beijing, where the least whisper at the centre can be heard right at the back, and vice versa. These places are marvels of acoustical engineering.

But the most beautiful man-made interior designed with its echo in mind is without doubt the medieval Gothic cathedral, the religious space *par excellence*, built to fulfil the spiritual needs of members of a community. Such holy places were designed to echo joyously when filled with the voices of the faithful. From certain parts of the choir in particular, the sound of the human voice is carried up into the tallest vaults. The soaring columns and pointed arches seem expressly designed to mirror the sounds that rise up between stone walls whose very structure seems to defy gravity. Seen from the outside, this miracle of architecture towers above the surrounding landscape, the towers and spires seeming to strain towards the heavens in the manner of the voices within.

In these special places of worship, no matter whether they have been chosen or built, the elemental purity of the *a capella* voice remains the most perfect form of human expression. Treating his body as a musical instrument, the singer modulates his vocal cords, using the breathing technique best suited to the nature of the piece. The mouth cavity itself can be used to produce certain sound effects, for example to create harmonics, wherever this is required by the repertoire.

The interiors of medieval churches and cathedrals have a resonance particularly suited to the sound of voices raised in song. Abbaye Saint-Georges-de Boscherville (Seine-Maritime).

Angelic choirs

Detail of *Virgin with Child, surrounded by angelic musicians*, known as
Madonna with Orchestra, by Giovanni Boccati; painting on wood, 1447.
National Gallery of Umbria, Perugia

Amplified by the vaulted interior spaces of the Gothic cathedral, *a capella* voices
are transformed, soaring upwards in competition with the grandeur of the
architecture.

When angels appear in paintings, it is because the concept of their celestial
voices is evocative of a dimension beyond the merely human. They are made to
look like asexual, ageless human beings, that is to say free of all worldly taint,
and haloed. Their wings suggest their role as messengers and mediators.
Listening to or playing music is meant to echo the example of the angels, being
a mode of expression that mediates between the purely human and the
immaterial dimension to which humanity aspires: the soul.

Sounds by their very nature rise upwards, impalpable, invisible, yet charged
with an emotional content that is at once tangible and impossible to describe.
They require a fitting external appearance, a materiality that is imbued with the
metaphysical, in which music and spiritual grace abound. Angels may be
compared to sounds; they transmit human aspirations and divine influence from
one world to the other.

The concert represented here combines song with instruments such as the
lute, with rhythmic, accompaniment from the cymbals and tambourine. It
expresses all the joy of the Nativity, and the musical accord of the instruments
that are regarded as the embodiments of harmony on heaven and earth.

Ethnic voices

Clearly the voice is the most personal expression of individuality. It is specific to the individual, instantly recognizable, and it is based on a person's particular way of speaking and physical make-up. But there are also cases where defined social groups who speak the same language, or are related in terms of physical characteristics, hold certain vocal attributes in common. Thus, within an ethnic group, there may be one type of voice, or several types, which it would be impossible to confuse with those of another ethnic grouping.

These particularities result of course from the physical characteristics of the ethnic group, which provide the basis of a distinctive vocal intonation – in the same way as their language itself is distinctive. Linguistic aptitudes have an influence on spoken or sung vocal emission, being dependent on the internal physical make-up of each individual, which itself is influenced by the immediate environment. Physical types are by nature many and varied, in just the same way as variations occur in the relief of a landscape, the regional climatic conditions or among local flora and fauna. The individual is born of a precise milieu, and is inevitably conditioned by the geographical factors of that milieu, as much by the sounds occurring all around as by his or her personal make-up. The sounds that any

individual attempts to emit will be the product of that overall equation.

Particular sorts of songs therefore constitute the distinctive mode of expression of different ethnic groups. They not only reflect the natural and biological order but also the social order, being for example community or responsorial songs, for a single voice or polyphonic with overlapping parts, refrain or ostinato. Elsewhere, more tuneful solo singing will tend to be favoured, with a broader melodic and vocal range and attempts at harmonics and diaphony. Elsewhere again, the mode of the sung emission may be reduced to the notes of a limited musical scale, a sort of chanting in which the individual gives voice to a narrative improvisation, relating his experiences and the incidents of his life – stories of hunting and fishing, travellers' tales, lamentations, accounts of historical or other events. Sung expression – whether in a massed group, in a circle, alone facing a group, as a response, or in isolation – will always be a reflection of social structure.

Where the individual finds himself isolated, in solitary contemplation of the vastness of nature, then a single voice, enhanced with all sorts of melodic variations, will suffice on its own to fill up the space. It will reflect precisely the condition of the singer's life – his loneliness, but also his freedom – in long songs and epics. Such songs are themselves evocative of the spaces in which they have their

Preceding double page: Singing is an intense and intimate musical experience. Children's choir in Shanghai (1949).

Below: Accompanying himself on the *morinkhuur*, the musician develops long phrases of sung melody, telling of legends and epic tales set in the vast plains of Inner Mongolia.

origins: broad horizons, legends filled with rides across the steppes, nomadic peoples moving over vast plains, jousting on horseback.... Elsewhere, community life will impose more intimate genres on the repertoire, in which the voices respond to each other, and communication between people occurs in the form of dialogues and exchanges. Here solidarity is more important than freedom.

Vocal and instrumental timbres: symbiosis

Curiously, the timbre of an instrument always resembles vocal timbre. In whatever country of the world, whatever differences may exist in terms of skill, technology and the materials used, the two will always seem to be mysteriously in accord. This will be the case, it seems, whatever the local circumstances, whether the voice provides the model, or whether the opposite occurs and it is the sounds of the musical instruments that guide the voice, or whether natural elements, such as the environment, climate, the local flora or the means of subsistence, for example, constitute the determining factors.

Nothing reveals the originality and spirit of a people better than this astonishing symbiosis. Inherent in the musical expression belonging to a culture is everything that contributed to its history and conditioned the very abilities that enabled it to survive and organize itself as a society. To a greater degree than any other cultural phenomenon, music represents the united voice of a population, the summation of its past history, the particular colour of its inflections and language.

Listening to Mongolian chants, how can one distinguish between the sound of the human voice and that of the *morinkhuur* viol with horse's head? Their voices are in unison, in respect of timbre and modulation, caught up in the same melodic undulations, the same leaps and bounds in which the ecstatic journey is accomplished. It is that quest which dictates both the subject of the epic tale and the form of the zoomorphic instrument, as well as the materials of which it is made. In the final reckoning, is it possible to break down the elements of this coherent whole, evolved over a long period of cultural gestation, culminating in a particular and unique sound which invokes, over and above the words of the song and the melody, the infinity of the open spaces that engendered them and, through them, the unknowable soul of a people?

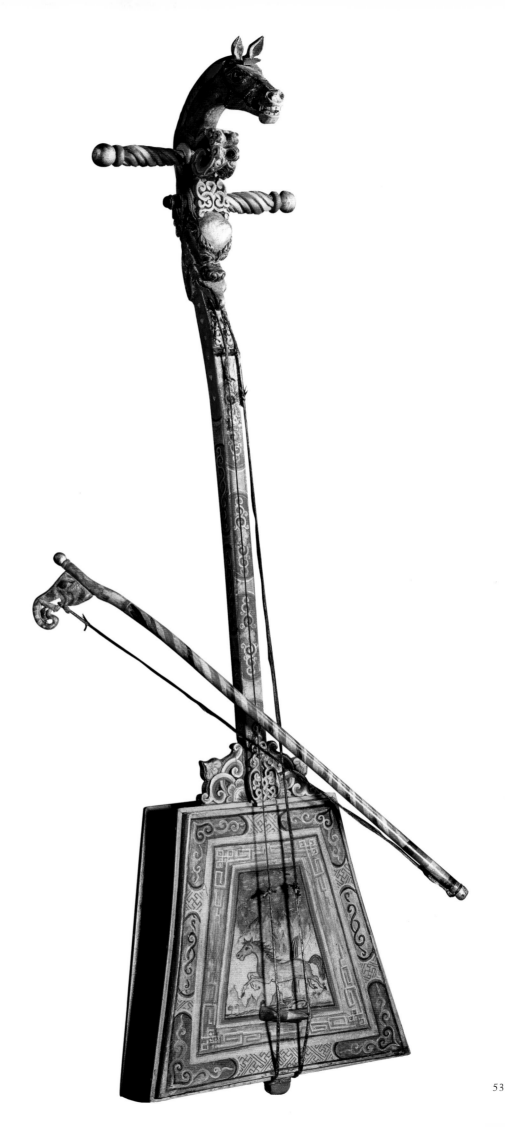

Morinkhuur fiddle belonging to the Khalkha, a nomadic people of Mongolia. The ornamental pegbox, the horsehair strings and bow together with the decoration of the soundbox, all serve to demonstrate that the instrument has its roots in a nomadic society dominated by horses. L. 120 cm (47¼ in.).

53

Distortions, imitations and sound effects

According to some Chinese sources, singing is the result of drawing out words – something that can better be imagined in the context of a polytonal language, in which the melodic line does not run counter to the speech tones but on the contrary amplifies and declaims them, stretching them to form held notes and more ornate sounds.

Many vocalizations, however, seem to have little to do with the words being spoken. Their various sound effects, distortions and inventions are more a matter of musical experimentation than sublimated language. Whistles, lisps, quavers, nasal sounds, hisses, clicks of the tongue and other such effects demand a sort of creative ingenuity similar to that required for the invention of musical instruments. Often noises emitted from the mouth require accessories such as improvised mirlitons – membranes or found materials used to modify the voice or

its timbre in the manner of a kazoo. Of the same order are such practices as striking the glottis to produce tremolo or vibrato effects, or puffing out the cheeks to produce sounds similar to those of the earliest instruments. In addition there is the whole gamut of rhythmic effects produced in these different ways, whether or not designed to articulate separate syllables, so that percussion too may legitimately be included among the range of vocal mechanisms.

Another voice-modifying device is the sound-intensifier or megaphone, often used to express suprahuman, theatrical voices belonging to beings of exceptional stature. Here once again we encounter that preoccupation with resonance that is so fundamental to the making of all musical instruments. In its simplest form, this most basic of instruments involves the use of one or both hands, with open palm, held against the mouth.

This use of the mouth both as a source of sound and as a resonator, whether amplified or not, is fundamental to the development of widely used instruments as the jew's harp or the musical bow, early ancestor of the entire chordophone family.

Playing the musical bow in Zimbabwe. The curved wooden arc held by the instrumentalist between his teeth communicates the vibrations of the playing string to the inside of his mouth, which not only serves as a resonator but also varies the volume.

Bodily rhythms

The history of body movements and their accompanying rhythms follows a very different course. Clapping the hands remains one of the most ancient gestures, bringing into play those eminently effective mechanisms for producing sound, the palms when struck one against the other (or one struck by the closed fingers of the other hand). All over the world, this quasi-spontaneous gesture, the sound of which varies according to the positions of the hands, provides the most common rhythmic accompaniment to the voice, as well as being used to show enthusiasm in the form of applause – an instinctive action which has an invigorating effect on the whole body by stimulating parts that are especially sensitive. After or during a musical performance, this idiophonic beating brings the listener's body into the experience and helps to release the pent-up energy aroused by the music and the rhythm.

Another widespread practice consists in striking the hands against other parts of the body, used directly as resonators. Certain traditional dances, notably in the Tyrol and in Spain, include the slapping of the thighs which, like clapping the hands or clicking the fingers, as in the *palmas* in Spanish dancing, is principally used for the purpose of

marking time, both by the dancers and by the spectators. These sounding gestures, rooted in rhythm and hence in dance, are most often used to accompany a tune, but they may exist independently as sequences in their own right where sounds and tempo alone are sufficiently eloquent to be regarded as music.

In certain ritual dances performed in Central Asia, Africa and Oceania, the chest or arm may be struck with a degree of force explicable only by a state of trance in which, possessed by the rhythm, groups of dancers beat one another until the blood flows and they lose consciousness. There are stories from all over the world that include incidents in which striking the abdomen is significant. Sometimes the tail of a mythical creature strikes its own belly, as in ancient Chinese legends about the Thunder Beast; or, as we learn from Vedic texts in India, the skin of a sacrificed animal may be beaten with the tail of the same animal. Among the Incas, the flayed ventral skin from the defeated enemy was beaten, in the manner of a drum. This use of ventral skin as a primitive membranophone features in many different traditions, prefiguring the construction of membrane drums, involving the use of stretched skin in a context quite separate from the human or animal body from which it was taken.

Above: Among the Mekeo people of South-East New Guinea, the lizard skin used to cover the *kundu* drum is struck directly with the fingers, which are used here as the percussive elements.

Double page overleaf: The gesture of the hand moved rapidly against the mouth can be observed in many parts of Africa, as seen here among the Samburu people of Kenya. The continuous emission of these woman's high-pitched cries is transformed by this means into a long-drawn-out wailing sound (ululation).

Vocal vibrato

Singing with vibrato and clapping of hands, Nineveh, Iraq. Detail of an
Assyrian bas-relief, c. 660–650 BC, discovered in 1850 by A.H. Layard.
British Museum, London

The achievement of vocal vibrato by beating the throat is among the most
ancient and most universal of rhythmic and acoustic practices. This freedom
to alter the timbre of the voice represented a new awareness of the musical
potential of the human body. It suggests also a knowledge of advanced vocal
techniques going beyond the simple voice production required for recitation,
psalmody or chant. Like many other voice-modifying procedures, it is rooted
in a belief in the magical origin of song: in Western civilization, the notion
of 'natural' song goes back no further than the Renaissance, when the
secularization of music began. In other parts of the world, however, song has
retained its sacred significance, and makes use of a variety of phonetic
resources such as whistles, cries, sounds made through closed lips and
clucking noises, to copy the widest possible range of registers and timbres,
way beyond the defined range of any one instrument. Echoing a musical
instrument in its modulations has in a certain sense impoverished the voice,
which has an infinite potential for sound effects and imitation. As it has
ceased to model itself on spoken elocution, song in the Western world has
followed an instrumental destiny and accommodated itself to a situation
where the search for melody has taken over from the ancient unity of song,
language and music.

Barefoot on the sacred earth

It would be hard to imagine a more primitive form of music than stamping on the ground. The deeply symbolic ritual act of treading the earth affirms the relationship of human beings to their native soil. In this act of appropriation of the earth trampled underfoot, man shows himself capable for the first time of expressing and externalizing the regular rhythm of his heart-beat, using his feet in a dance movement that is essentially an expression of joy translated into rhythm. Pulsating rhythms lie at the very heart of the human experience, and it is to translate and sublimate them that man leaps in the air and dances, transmitting his own internal vibrations to the ground below.

Without the use of any type of instrument to mediate between him and the ground, the dancer's body communicates directly, through his feet, with the yielding surface that offers itself up to the infinite possibilities of his physical movement and his imagination. Barefoot on the sacred earth, the North American Indian describes circles and rings, in the image of the earth. He belabours it with ritual dances when he prepares for the hunt or for combat, as though trying to communicate with it and by sheer repetition recover the primordial power of life it once breathed into him. The dervish gyrating on his axis echoes the rotation of the earth and taps the sources of creative

vibration. A spontaneous expression of movement, dance is more than a religious act, it is a rhythmic release of energy, an ecstatic act, a means of abandoning the self entirely in order to approach and become at one with the divinity.

Whatever the origin or purpose of dancing, the gestures of which it is composed and the movement that animates it, while they may not require musical support, do need the affirmation of rhythm. Sometimes that rhythm is amplified. One means of achieving greater resonance is to hollow out the surface and cover the space created with a floor. At the same time, the dancer may avail himself of footwear that is designed to make a loud noise – shoes with heels in the case of the flamenco dancer, and in other cases tap shoes.

The bell man

Sometimes the body itself is metamorphosed into an instrument, more especially a rhythm instrument. Decorations for the head, ears and arms, also belts, ankle-rings and knee-rings, are transformed during the dance into a rhythmic accompaniment that faithfully translates the slightest movement or vibration of the body into sound. These bells, spherical bells, rattling necklaces, head-dresses, leg-bands or knee-bands would originally have been made of natural materials, as for example the belts worn by Shuara women living in Amazonian Ecuador, east of the Andes; these produce a loud and brilliant sound, being composed of shells of freshwater molluscs, used in combination with seeds. The sound produced depends entirely on the type of shell used. Some emit more of a soft hiss, while the leg- and ankle-bells used as adornment by the Bamileke of Cameroun are made with halves of dried seeds which, when shaken, produce a noise like gurgling water.

Again in Ecuador, the Shuara use quite sophisticated natural materials, making earrings, for example, out of the hard outer wing-cases of beetles, which produce a rustling sound. Other acoustic ornaments are made from the beaks of toucans, threaded on strings together with the shells of river snails and seeds. Dried tree-leaves, banana among others, can be used as part of this dual-purpose decoration, particularly in necklaces and grass skirts. Sometimes the whole costume may consist of such plant material, as in the case of the covering worn during rain-making ceremonies in parts of Central America. Sometimes the body is covered with bushes of dried leaves, as among the Pygmies of Central Africa. In India, there is a garment made entirely of stones. A lot of other unexpected materials are used today for acoustic ornaments of this type, such as strung beads, coins, spherical and clapperless bells, rings etc. Ornamented in this way, the dancer is transformed into a musical instrument. He is now both man and bell, and moves his body to create sound or beat a rhythm. The tinkling of his ornaments is actually far more important than the gestures of the dance or any sort of rudimentary choreography. Being free to improvise, the dancer-musician sets the tone of the ceremony, and the assembled group is caught up in the rhythm he establishes. His body is an instrument but the music it produces is not pre-planned; rather it arises spontaneously from mediumistic practices.

Preceding double page: Dance performed by the Kwakiutl Indians in British Columbia, Canada, at the time of a solar eclipse. In order to ensure that the moon will be saved, the Kwakiutl chant incantations while dancing in a ring around a brazier. Photograph by Edward S. Curtis (1910).

Left: Leg movements form the basis of the ritual dance *intore* performed by the Tutsi of Rwanda. As the dancer stamps on the ground with his feet, the bells on his ankles to tinkle in time with his movements (c. 1970).

Double page overleaf: Whether it is the whirling dervishes of Egypt or the flamenco dancers of Spain, the movement of the performers is accentuated by the spectacular sight of their swirling garments.

Instruments worn on the body

Knee-plate consisting of a tortoiseshell that is attached to the dancer's leg; from it is suspended a 'rosary' composed of hinds' hooves which produces a rustling sound accompanying the movements of the dance and marking its rhythms. Arizona, United States. W. 8 cm (3¼ in.).

Pair of ankle-chimes or (*goun-grou*), made of small bells and metal spheres attached to an elaborate plaited cord. The tinkling of the bells emphasizes the dancer's foot movements, which correspond to the metre of the singer's words and the rhythm laid down by other percussion instruments, among them cymbals and drums of various types. Rajasthan, India. D. 8 cm (3¼ in.).

Shoulder belt (*txu*) made of tinkling ornaments, consisting of stalks of calabash gourds sewn onto a strip of cloth in thirty-six groups of miniature 'bells'. It is worn bandolier-fashion by men running relay races and to emphasize the movements of the body during dancing. Kraho Indians of Brazil. L. 74 cm (29¼ in.).

Clappers, rattles and sistra

Concerned to make his rhythmic gestures louder and more emphatic, man soon moved on from objects simply worn to objects used as extensions of his body. Idiophonic instruments of this type were held in both hands and clashed together to produce sounds; they were therefore by definition objects used in pairs, and most frequently made of the same material: two stones, two sections of branch, two plant shells, two mollusc shells, etc.

Prehistoric wall paintings in Australia attest to the antiquity of the practice among aborigines of hitting two sticks together, a percussive technique still employed by their descendants to accompany their dances, together with other forms of rhythmic accompaniment such as striking the ground with a stick and blowing into a 'megaphone' or didgeridu. Ivory clappers in the shape of human hands, from Ancient Egypt, and curved plates designed to be clashed together, dating from the Sumerian period (3rd millennium BC), are examples of other ancient objects related to instruments still in use among the Australian aborigines, these resembling a boomerang in form. Wooden clappers of this type, engraved and sculpted in particularly elaborate fashion, are still used by the Bozo of Upper Niger. Their manufacture and use complies with a complex set of mythological and social requirements, reflecting the importance of their ritual role.

The ancient gesture of hollowing the hands and clapping them together gave rise to instruments that reflected this arrangement, reminiscent of a bivalve, of hands coming into collision. Among these are castanets, cymbals, crotalums and also the individual elements of sistra such as the *wasamba*, a type made of calabash sections threaded onto a stick.

Also conceived as rhythmic extensions of the hands are objects requiring manipulation such as rattles and other shaken instruments, sistra, bells etc. For preference, these will be made up of elements that already produce sounds when used individually – and indeed it is quite often the case that such instruments merely make different use of items originally adopted as acoustic ornaments. It is for example possible to make a sistrum by suspending from a stick or frame elements that will bang together, such as

sections of calabash or pieces of metal, or, equally, to attach a wooden handle to the end of a gourd-bell, or pierce a gourd-bell with a stick to make a rattle. And indeed there are certain gourds whose natural shape makes them so easy and convenient to hold that they do not even require the addition of a handle.

An almost infinite number of plant shells exist in various forms, ranging from calabashes to the fruit of the baobab tree. When shaken, these produce a vast range of individual sounds, depending on the type of dried seeds trapped inside, which collide with the inner wall. The container may also be an animal bladder, or even be made of wickerwork.

If the fruit takes too long to dry out on the inside, it is possible to empty out the seeds and replace them with small pebbles or balls of clay, which rattle against the walls in exactly the same way. Other materials are chosen for their sacred qualities, since rattles are often reserved for magical purposes. The materials employed may vary depending on

Preceding double page: Dance performed by the wives of the king among the Podokwo in the far north of Cameroun. As the dancers advance in single file, their steps are accompanied by the tinkling of bells worn on their ankles.

Opposite: *Mbuya* dance performed by the Bapende of the Democratic Republic of Congo. The dancers' arm movements are emphasized by the sounds produced by the bell rattle, while their leg movements are accompanied by the tinkling of ankle bells.

Left: *Wasamba* sistrum of the Bambara in Mali, made of sections of calabash gourd threaded onto a V-shaped stick. Use of this instrument is associated with circumcision rituals for young boys. L. 35 cm (13¾ in.).

the circumstances. If, for example, the witch doctor wants to cure an illness, he may use an inedible gourd inside which he has placed beetles or other insects instead of the customary small seeds. In other cases, where rattles are supposed to be used to accompany singing or to serve as instruments to welcome a guest, then a particular variety of calabash will be used. Elsewhere, in certain of their fertility rites, the Inuit people of the Arctic throw the bladders of seals and walruses into the sea. Certain rattles can be enclosed inside a net, to which are affixed, depending on the circumstances, the stones of fruits, cowrie shells or snake vertebrae. In response to being shaken, these external elements strike the gourd at the same time as the contents rattle around inside, thus causing two independent sound sources to emit vibrations, internally and externally.

The addition of a handle, a crossbar or a frame to support the acoustic elements marks a fundamental step in the evolution towards vibrations of different types. The instruments in question are no longer under the direct and immediate influence of the hand, but are shaken by means of the bodily extension. With the action transferred in this way, it is possible for all the various rhythms of the hands, feet and body to be superimposed polyrhythmically. There is also the potential for auditory dissociation, as the listener's attention is transferred in turn from the timbre of one sound to another, or to the gestures or to the cadences of the whole.

The rhythm stick

Whether it is the use of hollow bamboo canes to pound the ground and thus produce rhythmic sounds, as in the Fiji Islands or in Taiwan, or of spears to beat time on the island of New Britain in Papua New Guinea, the rhythm stick that serves to mark the beat or tempo of a dance – but which can also be used as a tool or support, sceptre, wand or magical repository of good medicine – must be accounted one of the very simplest types of indirect percussion instruments in existence, and also one of the most widely distributed throughout the world.

Essentially we are back in the musical tradition of the feet stamping on the ground, whether or not assisted by soles designed to accentuate the rhythmic beat, as for example, clogs, tap shoes or the Hawaiian device of the swinging wooden flap, all of which make use of the same principle of percussion.

These rhythm pipes and rhythm sticks are usually hollowed out and function as resonators. The pipes that are pounded against the ground may be blocked at one or other end, either naturally so in the case of the nodes of a bamboo cane, or by the use of wax. This gives a different sound depending on whether the open or closed end is brought into contact with the ground. Their length, calibre and dimensional variations all have an influence on the nature of the resulting sound.

In the same way, the kind of surface that absorbs the impact is crucial: the rhythm stick can hit the ground directly, or may strike a plank or block, or hit the bottom of a cavity. Based on the same principle is the practice of

Group of Zulu girls tribe brandishing long bamboo canes that symbolize lances. As the girls advance in close formation, the canes clash and set up a continuous rattle. South Africa, Nongoma (Natal province).

producing particular sounds by beating a hollow tree-trunk, or a trunk in which holes have been made, using sticks of variable diameter and length, and the pounding of troughs and mortars by means of hollow pipes of different formats. A close relative of the rhythm stick is the *angklung* from Java or the Solomon Islands; in this instrument the pipes – two or three in number and of different heights, set vertically inside a frame – are designed to swing against the rim of a wooden gutter.

Because of similarities in structure and method of percussion, the rhythm stick inevitably makes one think of a closely related instrument, the wooden drum. In the absence of a membrane, it is the carcass itself that is beaten, on the edge of a slit that opens into the interior of the hollow instrument. The main difference is that in this situation the sound source is reversed. It is now the object that is being struck, rather than the object that does the hitting, that acts as the resonator.

Tree drums

A hollow tree-trunk, regarded in some traditions as a residence for spirits, is a particularly good carrier of sound when used as a slit drum. The wooden drum represents the body of primitive man, it is both tree of life and ancestor, echoing phallus as well as symbol of fertility and power. It is also the receptacle of potential life, either in the form of seeds or blood poured into it during sacrificial ceremonies. Like a womb, it holds life within it, and it can transmit resonances, cries, appeals and messages. It is by its very nature ideal for accompanying dance and song, but it can also fulfil the role of sending out signals, summonses and alarms, the characteristic low sound frequencies of the slit

drum making it particularly suitable for transmitting information over long distances.

After experimenting with the different pitches which these tree-trunks were capable of producing, sometimes hollowing them out by lighting fires, or depositing embers or red-hot stones inside them, men then attempted to give them shape and form. Wooden drums such as these exhibit extremely variable dimensions. Once felled, the tree-trunks were laid flat on the ground to be worked on, or they could be suspended over a pit, which helped the sound to carry, or supported at an oblique angle between two stakes. On occasion they rested on lugs left intact by the workman when stripping off the branches.

Most have a slit that runs along their length, and this may be anything from a simple aperture with two lips of unequal thickness, to two tongues coming from opposite sides; others have communicating holes, square, round or triangular in section.

The tall upright drums of the type seen in the New Hebrides and in parts of Africa, known as 'drum trees', are sometimes phallic in form and have a longitudinal slit at the mid-point, which the indigenous peoples describe as the vulva of the instrument.

Traditionally made from a section of tree-trunk having a girth similar to that of a human body and approximately 1 metre (3 ft) in length, the Mexican drum *teponazli* has an H-shaped aperture in the form of two tongues which, struck, produce harmonic vibrations of the fundamental note of the main trunk. The instrument may take the form of a two-headed creature, of human or animal origin, sometimes with the appearance of a monkey, at other times bearing the heads of snakes or caymans – the word *coatl* in the language of the Aztecs means both 'snake' and 'twin'. There are mythological associations relating to the 'earthly' or 'rainy' nature of these animals. This drum is depicted in a

Opposite: Wooden drum hollowed out of a section of tree-trunk. Musical instruments of this type are found on all five continents, in a variety of different forms. They are used principally to accompany dancing and to send messages. Bubaque, Bijagós archipelago, Guinea-Bissau.

Below: Wooden drum of the *teponazli* type, with two tongues coming from opposite sides, known as *macuilxochitl* (Mexico). The body is sculpted in low relief and depicts the Mexican god of music, Macuilxochitl. L. 52 cm (20½ in.); D. 14 cm (5½ in.).

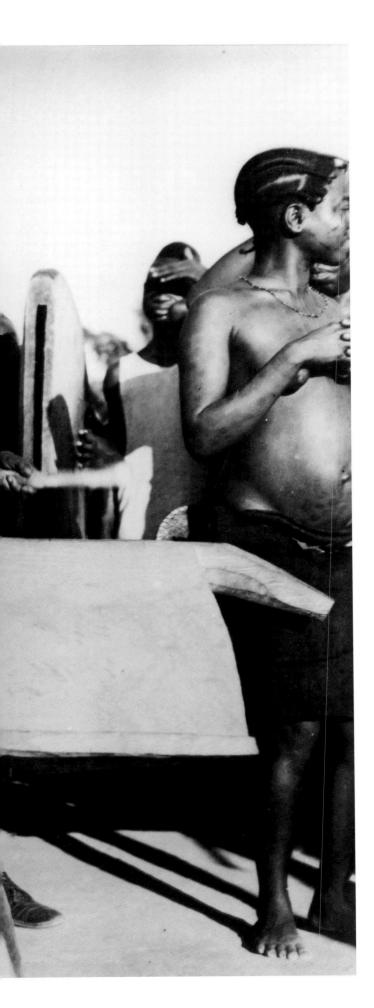

carved relief on the Great Temple of Tenochtitlán in Mexico. It was included as part of the booty at the time of the victory of Axayacatl (1469–81) over neighbouring Tlatelolco. The instrument would be placed near the sovereign's ashes and was used as a support on which to perform the ritual human sacrifice (by cutting out the heart) of the servants whose destiny it was to accompany the deceased king into the afterlife. It also had sacrificial blood poured over it when a new sovereign acceded to the throne. A cult object and a receptacle of energy, it was regarded as the personification of the divinity brought to life during sacrificial ceremonies. The well-being of the whole community depended upon it.

The slit drums of the Jivaro Shuara are used in connection with initiation rites for boys entering manhood – hence the numerous proscriptions attached to their manufacture and the persons allowed to approach the instrument. The type of wood employed is associated with the element of water and the world of the dead, being also used for the manufacture of canoes, coffins and ceremonial seats, all of which are decorated at one end (both in the case of the drum) with the heads of reptiles. The slit of the instrument is of a zigzag form approximating to a snake's body. The drum is inhabited by Arutam, the spirit of the waterfall where the initiation is performed; the boys call on it with all sorts of noises and vocal sounds, and the drum is supposed to sound like rushing water. When being played, it is suspended obliquely between two stakes, and beaten on the top as well as the bottom.

Impressive both for its dimensions – about 3.50 metres (11 ft 6 in.) long in the case of the example in the Musée de l'Homme in Paris – and for its spectacular decoration, the big *avokwe* drum of the Ebrie people of the Ivory Coast is carved from the wood of the sacred tree the *iroko*, which is an especially hard timber that does not rot. The method of choosing the tree to be used for the manufacture of the drum is a particularly solemn procedure. After consultation with the 'sayer of hidden things', sacrifices are offered to the spirits who inhabit the chosen tree. The felling, cutting up and transportation are performed collectively, with the whole community mobilized for the task. Once the drum has been carved and consecrated with a bloody sacrifice, it is given its name and entrusted to the drum-keeper charged with its care and use.

The two lips of the drum are of the same thickness but follow arcs of different lengths. One emits a low sound, the other a sound of higher pitch. Each of the ends is extended by means of a board. On one stands a sculpture of a leopard holding a white-painted figure in its claws, flanked by three severed heads wearing head-dresses and a double row of human jawbones. At the other end, three severed heads are displayed with a double row of maxillae. The body of the drum is decorated with black-and-white geometric motifs painted in blood and kaolin.

Just as it was customary to suspend from the drum trophies consisting of the skulls and jawbones of enemies killed in war or sacrificed during captivity, so too were enemy skulls and weapons deposited under the canopy used to shelter the drum. The instrument was placed over a ditch

Left: The drummer uses this magnificent wooden drum, cut from a single block in the shape of a stylized animal, for playing melodic and rhythmic sequences to accompany dancing or for sending messages over long distances. Mayogo people of the Democratic Republic of Congo.

Overleaf: In some parts of China, separating the chaff from the wheat is done by shaking a wickerwork sieve with a prescribed ritual gesture. As the grain slides about and falls back into the sieve, it produces a series of sounds that form a musical accompaniment.

that amplified the resonance, which we know to have been considerable as the sound carried over distances if up to 20 kilometres (12 miles).

These few examples illustrate the important ritual and sacred role of the wooden drum, which was conceived of as a living being complete in every respect, with a sexual identity and a variety of functional attributes and uses. It was made from a distinct and identifiable element of nature – the tree – and the process of its manufacture was highly symbolic, carried out according to the precise rules established by the social group that created and utilized it. Nothing about the way it was used was left to chance, not its decoration, nor the place where it was kept, and certainly not the sound it produced.

Work rhythms

Dance directly incorporates the rhythms of instruments worn on the body or wielded by the dancer, but there are circumstances and practices that involve the wearing or carrying of instruments in every department of people's lives: work, play, clothing, habitat and sexuality. Sometimes the sounds produced will have been activated by chance, sometimes deliberately.

Many opportunities arise in the course of the daily round to include rhythm and music in the performance of tasks of all kinds, and even to subordinate the latter to the former. Rhythmic working provides collective and individual encouragement, whether it is articulated by means of the tools being used or by means of song accompanying the movements, matching its tempo to the pattern of breathing associated with the physical effort required by the task in hand. Whether or not the human body is used directly as an acoustic element, gesture and the noises that accompany it, as well as the effort that underlies it, all combine to create a repetitive dynamic in which sound assumes coherent form, begins to swell and ultimately takes shape as individual invention and an element of a repertory.

Music created in this way and based on work rhythms can survive in circumstances different to those of its conception, and indeed it may become an identifying feature of a particular ethnic group, possibly even the only trace of that people either to survive in the memory of native inhabitants or to be recognizable by strangers unfamiliar with the society. Such is the enduring power of creativity that it is able to survive alone and in time needs no other justification but itself. All that matters is its internal consistency and its originality as a composition. In it is revealed the genius of a culture, and its ability to express its own distinctive nature through music rooted in real activities which – albeit hard and repetitive – were nevertheless accepted as part of a common effort and therefore considered worthwhile. At the end of it, what will emerge is a song or melody that will for ever be viewed by the external world as a musical masterpiece and a unique cultural testimony.

These particular sound sequences may happen to serve as a source of inspiration for some poet or composer who has his own distinctive way of organizing them into music, or it may be that the singers and musicians themselves perfect their performance in a manner deserving of admiration. Not everyone has a Bela Bartók or a Komitas (1869–1935; the Armenian-born composer and specialist in folk music) to be their ears and to transcribe and preserve oral traditions in songs and poems.

All the infinite variety of essential tasks provide an extensive acoustic palette based on the materials used and the sounds they emit, as well as rhythms derived from the functional gestures appropriate to working in the fields – threshing, ploughing, sowing rice – or to craft or industrial tasks such as fulling cloth, smithing etc. One hypothesis is that the origin of the friction drum lies in the manipulation of the membrane of the bellows-type used in Ancient Egypt, and still in use today among the people inhabiting that region.

The sounds made by a number of other instruments, mostly idiophones, appear to be transpositions of the sounds characteristic of a particular kind of physical work: the ratchet rattle recalling the use of the grindstone; and the scraper, as its name suggests, relating to the culinary process of scraping or grating foodstuffs. A whole variety of materials are known to be used as musical scrapers; such instruments may be made of, *inter alia*, bone, reindeer antlers, spinal vertebrae, carapaces, shells, the jawbones of animals, calabashes, wooden or metal pipes with striations, and notched sticks.

The tintinnabulation of everyday life and activity

Many objects related to food and its preparation have been adapted for musical purposes. The beating of plates and bowls of more or less primitive form – made of such materials as pottery, calabash or metal, either inverted or placed above water to give a better sound – lies at the origin of many of the timpani and other percussion instruments which, like the Indian pottery that is such an effective carrier of sound, perform the orchestral function of membranophones (although they may also be used independently as accompaniments for singing and dancing). Glass bells, which became fashionable in the eighteenth century, were designed to produce the notes of a scale when rung or gently rubbed; this idea had its origins in sets of glasses or porcelain bowls which were filled with liquid and ranged in a semicircle in order of size, in the manner of a drum kit, the sound being produced by rubbing the vessels with sticks.

The domestic space and the urban environment generate a fair amount of music and sound in their own right. There are many items set in motion either manually or by the wind that are placed within or on the outside of dwellings – anything from the doorbell and doorknocker, or small bells that ring when someone enters, to mobiles suspended from the roof or ceiling. Sometimes their function is protective, designed to ward off evil influences, but they may also serve as summonses or signals, or to mark time or tell the hour. That is the role of the big bells and drums found in

Preceding page: The rhythmic cadence of the grindstone as it moves to and fro is reminiscent of the sounds and gestures of a musician playing a scraper.

Above: As the instrument is kept firmly pressed against the musician's mouth, the vibration of his lips is transmitted down into the interior of the long spiralling horn. The shape of each individual horn partly determines the timbre of sound produced. Masai tribe, Kenya.

Opposite: Harness made of tinkling ornaments, worn by a dancer in Papua New Guinea. Shells, small round bells and old bottle-tops chink together in time with the dancer's movements.

the Far East, placed on either side of the temple doors, or alternatively in two separate towers flanking the entrance gate of a town or citadel.

Apart from the acoustic ornaments and jewelry worn to accentuate the rhythm of a dance, a whole range of tinkling accessories is used in conjunction with apparel: small spherical bells sewn onto garments, charms, sequins, ornaments for the forehead and hair, acoustic rings, shards of glass, clinking chains for the arms or ankles to emphasize the movements of the body, not to mention the clacking of sandals or heels while walking; these ornaments are often worn to confer protection, and their brightness both of sound and appearance is thought to ward off the evil eye and wicked spirits.

Of the same order are certain jewels and acoustic objects attached to the bodies of children to keep them safe, and which often in fact have a dual function, being both an object to suck and bite and, perhaps, a rattle with the ability to exorcise spirits, a bull-roarer or a clapper drum with its whirling balls – toys to play with and at the same time instruments which in other circumstances are used only by the witchdoctor or local shaman. The list of such toys endowed with a protective function is a long one: they would in fact include most of the instruments used in ritual, such as ratchet rattles, clappers, humming tops, whistling vessels, conch shells, knucklebones, aeolian flutes and other whirring mirlitons attached to kites.

Body extensions

Clearly it is necessary for an instrument to be in close proximity to the musician's body, for it is a physical extension of his person – different, of course, because fabricated, and separate. At the end of a period of familiarization and adjustment on the part of the player, it holds out the prospect of a harmonious and fulfilling relationship. It is possible to imagine a variety of different sorts of instrumental extensions. The breath, for example, is extended into pipes and calamuses when these are raised to the mouth. The capacity for resonance is extended from the thoracic cavity or the stomach by means of resonators such as calabashes or coconut shells, which are held against those parts of the body as they are played. The tongue and its vibratory capability is extended by means of the primitive reed that consists of a leaf or blade of grass held in the fingers in front of the lips, by the tongue of the jew's harp or the string of the musical bow.

A harmonious relationship exists between the human body and the instrument, for the one cannot operate without the other. Without his instrument, a musician may be likened to an amputee or a rider without his horse. Both are made up of body and soul and together they become like two human beings whose identities merge in the playing. One has only to observe the actions of a violinist or guitarist to note the loving tenderness with which he or

she seems to caress the instrument, speak to it, coax sounds out of it, making it vibrate and respond with sweet melodies and eloquent phrases.

Instrumental anthropomorphism

The shape of instruments frequently shows clear signs of stylization based on the human body. The Cycladic figures of the protohistoric Mediterranean world seem to anticipate the feminine curves of the Western violin. A whole line of morphological descent can be traced back to ancient representations of the human female which emphasize the pubic triangle. Schematizations of the latter began with the shape of a heart and evolved gradually towards representations of a body with a pinched-in waist, progressively deprived of arms, and with the neck and head extended – a morphology characteristic of Cretan art of the 3rd millennium BC.

Instrumental anthropomorphism is almost always sexually differentiated. In the case of certain African harps of strikingly human form, the head is fashioned with considerable care, even down to the detail of the hairstyle, and while there is often a high degree of stylization, each head nevertheless retains its distinct personality and exhibits the characteristic features of its ethnic group. Certain harps represent the whole human body sculpted in the round, while in other cases only characteristic sexual features are made explicit.

In the case of chordophones, and in particular viols, the *gusla* and certain zithers of the Hummel or arpanetta type, a sculpted head is commonly shown with blindfolded eyes, and a torso not dissimilar to that of a ship's figurehead. The word 'zither' derives after all from the Greek *khitasis* meaning 'thorax', suggestive perhaps of a swelling chest.

Representations of the human body in whole or in part are characteristic of many of the membranophones, also some bell handles and external bell-clappers. Although certain instruments have a timbre that seems to correspond to either a male or a female voice, this aural association is often contradicted by their form. The flute, for example, with its eminently feminine high notes, always has phallic connotations, while the booming bass of the drum is generally linked to the female belly. This ambivalence expresses, in more or less clear proportions, a dualism that is inherent in human nature, as well as an ideal of complementarity as the basis of all harmony.

Other instruments directly suggest the sexual act, either by their form or by the manner in which they are played. The friction drum for example, which is played with a wooden rod, combines the female morphology of the container with the masculine form of the rod. The jew's harp also has strong erotic connotations, consisting as it does of a thin blade or tongue of steel, wood or bamboo that vibrates against the teeth, using the buccal cavity as a resonator. It has been used virtually all over the world as an instrument for performing serenades, and was actually banned in puritanical societies like that prevailing in nineteenth-century Vienna. In China and Vietnam it is still used today by lovers paying court.

Sometimes it is customary for a particular instrument always to be played by one or other of the sexes. There seems to be no universal law about this, and what is *de rigueur* in one country may be contradicted in another. While the flute is almost always restricted to male players, the drum is not the exclusive preserve of either sex. In some parts of the world the women play the drums, as for example the South American *bombo*, while elsewhere, and especially in Asia, it is very rare to see a female lay hands on this instrument. In precisely the same way, in the Western world, women were only relatively recently allowed access to the cello, percussion instruments and the organ. The instruments traditionally reserved for feminine use were those that did not involve too many contortions, such as the lute, the zither or a keyboard instrument, which allowed the player to be seated in a manner adjudged respectable.

Right: Five-stringed arched harp of the Zande people in the Democratic Republic of Congo. Under the harp's watchful eye, the strings link the 'neck' with the 'belly' of the instrument. Soundbox: L. 38 cm (15 in.); neck and carved head: L. 57 cm (22½ in.).

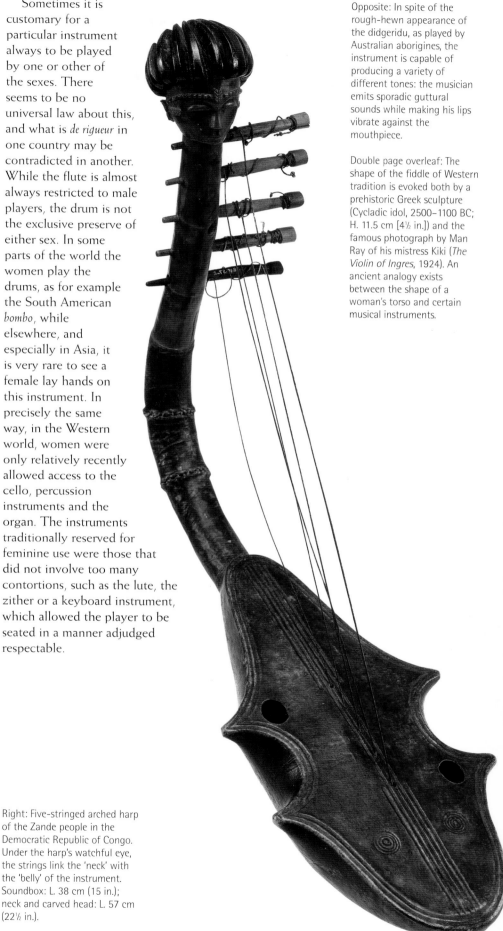

Opposite: In spite of the rough-hewn appearance of the didgeridu, as played by Australian aborigines, the instrument is capable of producing a variety of different tones: the musician emits sporadic guttural sounds while making his lips vibrate against the mouthpiece.

Double page overleaf: The shape of the fiddle of Western tradition is evoked both by a prehistoric Greek sculpture (Cycladic idol, 2500–1100 BC; H. 11.5 cm [4½ in.]) and the famous photograph by Man Ray of his mistress Kiki (*The Violin of Ingres*, 1924). An ancient analogy exists between the shape of a woman's torso and certain musical instruments.

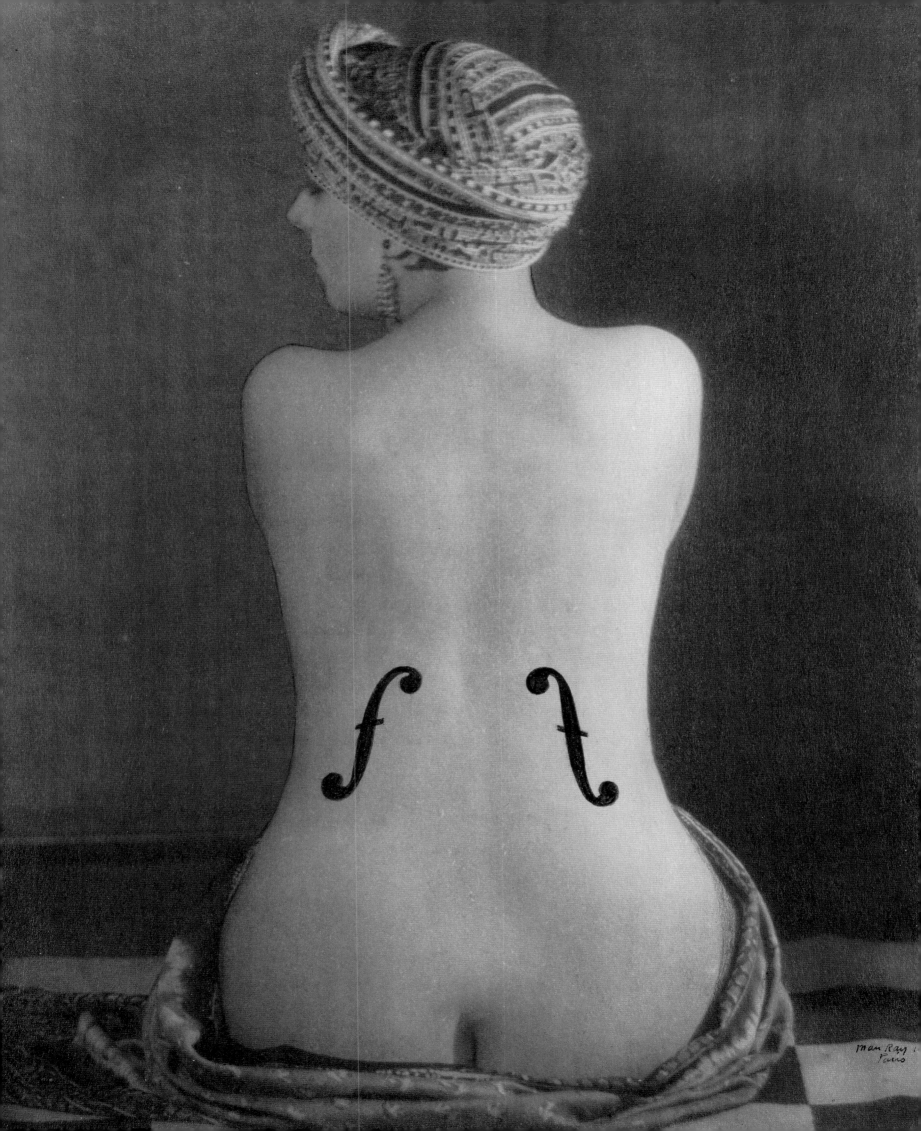

Anthropomorphism

Arched harp with six plant-fibre strings and a wooden soundbox. The flexed legs correspond to a dance position often represented in African statues. The expressive face is surmounted by a hairstyle with centre parting. Ngbaka people of the Lua basin, Democratic Republic of Congo. L. 81 cm (32 in.).

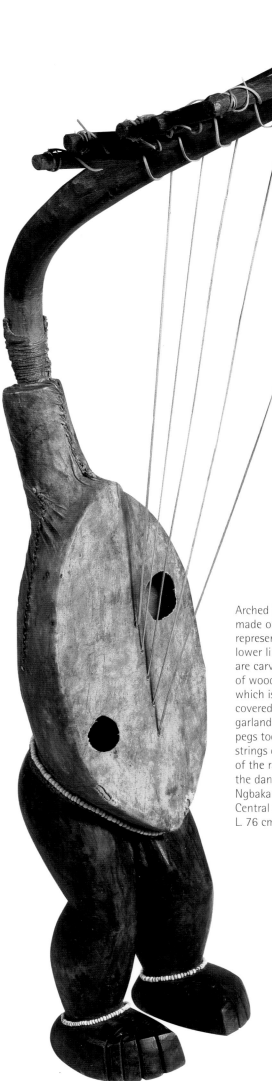

Arched harp with five strings made of plant fibre, representing a male figure. The lower limbs and the soundbox are carved from a single block of wood. The ovoid torso, which is hollowed out and covered with a skin, is garlanded with beads, and the pegs too are decorated with strings of beads, in the manner of the rattles often worn by the dancers of the region. Ngbaka of the Upper Ubangi, Central African Republic. L. 76 cm (30 in.).

Earthenware bell representing a woman, dating from Greek antiquity. The long neck serves as a handle, while the full dress forms the skirt of the bell and the legs serve as clappers. The function of this bell remains unknown, but given its extreme fragility, it is unlikely to have been used for musical purposes. Boeotia, Late Geometric period, 8th century BC.

Lamellaphone of the *sanza* type, with eleven thin strips of vegetable material on an anthropomorphized soundbox carved out of wood. The instrument is classified as a plucked idiophone, with a row of flexible bars attached to a soundbox. Cameroun. H. 32 cm (12½ in.); W. 16 cm (6¼ in.).

The musical bestiary

Other instruments are deliberately made to be zoomorphic. A large number of wooden drums are designed to represent animals that may be of virtually any species, from the ox to the cayman. A Chinese instrument called the *muyü*, or wooden fish, is used in Buddhist chanting. It consists of a hollowed out block of wood shaped and decorated like a fish, with a large semicircular aperture in the base.

Examples of board zithers made in the shape of a crocodile are found in Bangladesh and Burma, as well as among the instruments used in the Javanese gamelan. The metallophone *saron*, the Balinese *gansa gambang* or the *gender* may represent a dragon. A whole peacock complete with tail feathers constitutes the body of the Indian fretted lute, the *mayuri*. Scrapers too can be made to resemble a variety of different animals, from the tortoise to the tiger-box *yü*, a member of the Chinese orchestra.

Most wooden drums are representations, on a reduced or enlarged scale, of some legendary figure or ancestor, who is in the act of becoming one with the axis of the world and so establishing communication between Heaven and Earth.

Large wooden drums from Melanesia – phallus-shaped objects that are stood on end – exhibit the semblance of a face with a beak and, as with all wooden drums that have a single slit, two lips of unequal thickness that are capable of producing sounds in two different pitches, and which approximate in form to a vulva. The symbolic morphology is more significant than any semblance of realism, and the drums play an important role in the ritual performances of the population groups concerned. By displaying in exaggerated form their sexual hybridity and superhuman – or super-animal – qualities, they become mutant beings of indefinite and unclassifiable species, both part of the world because they are made up of identifiable elements, and alien to it because of the singular way in which these elements are combined.

Numerous earthenware whistles from Central America and Europe are made in the form of birds and function as bird-calls, in the same manner as animal-calls are used to imitate the sounds of species being hunted. The range of instruments from South America includes also whistles that are either anthropomorphic in form or represent animals or hybrid creatures, such as lizards, snakes and caymans, inspired by the gods of the Aztec pantheon.

Once again it is the links with founding deities, legendary figures or ancestors that are perpetuated, the line of descent and degree of relationship being emphasized jointly by the representational form and the voice of the particular instrument.

Corporeal denominations

It is perhaps no great surprise to learn that the bodily associations of instruments extend as well to the language in which they are described: for example, the neck, belly and waist, as well as the body of a guitar. This use of the names of parts of the human body sometimes goes way beyond physical appearance. Jadis Ziriab, principal musician at the

Wooden drum in the shape of a fish, suspended from the roof timbers within the precinct of a Buddhist temple in Korea.

court of the Abbasid caliph Harun al-Rashid (786–809), is said to have compared the strings of the *ud* with the four humours of man, and by extension the four temperaments: the highest string, painted yellow, represented the bilious; the second string, painted red, stood for the sanguinary; the white symbolized the phlegmatic; and the thickest, which was black, corresponded to the atrabilious, the seat of melancholy and anger. A fifth string was added, which was the soul, its task being to connect all the rest together and bring them to life.

Where instruments are concerned, vernacular speech tends to make the assumption that the body referred to is an ideal body, of a perfection to be emulated, perhaps the body of some celebrated hero of antiquity. The various elements of the *sarangi*, for example, are described in terms of human body parts: mouth, throat, belly, waist and hips are the words used. But, as in the Upanishads, it is the body of some sort of legendary figure, made in the image of a divine instrument – and not the other way round. The human instrument is in imitation of the divine instrument; as the latter has a head, so has the former, and in the same way as the latter has a belly, so does the former; as the latter has a tongue, so the former has a timbre; as the latter has fingers, so the former has strings, as the latter is covered in hairy skin, so too is the former …'.

In certain areas of the Far East, a very particular terminology is applied to the zither. The instrument is described using the names of the parts of the body belonging to a legendary creature, the dragon, which is supposed to have attained its ideal form in a series of mutations. Being made from selected materials, combining all the virtues of *yin* and *yang* in a harmonious whole, the dragon is the culmination of all animal and human tribulations, for it uniquely represents all the stages of evolution. The instrument in which it is materialized will thus possess all the qualities of the different realms of creation, and its voice will express perfection.

Human materials

The human body itself furnishes some of the elements required to make musical instruments: a male femur in the case of the Tibetan *rkang-gling*; the name means 'made of a man's leg'. This ritual trumpet was the prototype for similar instruments made of different materials, such as metal or animal horn. Again in

Tibet, the human cranium is used in making the *damaru*, a drum with whirling balls; here two skulls are combined and, according to the holy texts, it is preferable for these to be taken respectively from a boy of sixteen and a girl of twelve. Monkey skins are stretched over the skulls, and one end is decorated with an eight-petalled lotus smeared with a girl's menstrual blood, and the other end with a mandala. Sixteen pierced holes allow the skin to be attached using human hair. The whirling balls are made of bones taken from a waterbird's foot and encased in wax and cloth.

Human bones are used in the shaman's apron that rattles as he performs his rhythmic dance. Other instruments such as the gourd rattle may be covered with a net to which vertebrae are attached, while teeth are frequently used in acoustic necklaces. The membranes of drums are sometimes of human origin, but most often they are made of animal skin, chosen specifically to represent a particular entity or to make that entity speak through the instrument. Human hair and horsehair are used for bows, notably that of the viol with horse's head, the *morinkhuur*, the preferred 'mount' of the Mongolian shaman.

The use of materials taken from human bodies has magical implications, linking the human, animal, vegetable and mineral worlds in an indissociable whole. By taking possession of these elements and controlling them in his own way, according to a logic and a desire that are his and his alone, man expresses his vision of the world. He organizes his universe by filling it with bodies and voices.

Opposite: Man playing the *sarangi* fiddle in Jodhpur, Rajasthan. The vernacular terms used in India to designate the different parts of the *sarangi* correspond to those used for the human body. It thus has a mouth, belly, hips etc.

The *damaru* drum, used in Tibetan Buddhist ritual. This instrument is made of two human skullcaps (one male, the other female) joined at the top. H. 17 cm (6¾ in.); D. 14 cm (5½ in.).

3   Religious and Ritual Uses

When soul becomes symphony

Music is and always has been the universal vehicle of man's attempts to reach out to a higher dimension of reality. Sounds are the means by which he makes the leap into the unknown. To communicate with the intangible other world that lies just beyond his reach, it is necessary to transcend the material substance, so that no physical obstacle stands in the way of the divine influence.

Matter as mediator

Subjugating material reality, making it tractable, one might even say annihilating it – that is the challenge faced by the instrument maker, the shaman or the musician. The musical instrument in the making is fashioned from elements taken from everyday life – things drawn from man's environment and which he has learned empirically to manipulate by the adoption of more or less complicated techniques. Apprehending the material world solely in terms of its sounds has the effect of rendering it insubstantial, so that it becomes no more than a vibration in the air, accessible to the ear alone.

The concept of the Tree of Life is common to all societies, being seen variously as a channel for the life-force, a living, growing root, a ladder of initiation, a haunt of spirits and a resting place of the gods. By touching it, one is imbued with its powers; when stroking it one is aware of its voice, when one penetrates inside it, seeking refuge, it is like returning to the maternal womb. Hence that primal urge to search out hollow trees, to elicit sounds from them, to get inside them and stand on the axis of the world, to rediscover lost echoes and secret myths – all of which actions give rise to the creation of magic drums, sounding trees, and tribal totem poles. Because of its shape, the interior of a hollow tree-trunk has the potential to serve

as coffin or cradle, crucible of energies, trophy chest or drum. In fact it is all of these things: source, receptacle and echo chamber.

Fundamental to man's attempts to dominate or at the very least to placate the forces of nature is the need to establish an analogy between nature and instrument, based on their common origin. Once the concept that all things are interrelated is acknowledged, and that each one affects the rest at every level in the relationship of cause and effect, then the magical principle is established which states that it is only necessary to influence one part of the whole in order to extend that influence to the totality.

It is the imitation of voices, vocal timbres and calls, along with the copying of behaviour, appearance and displays, that puts music and its complementary form, dance, at the forefront of such endeavours. The instruments employed function as the means not only of emitting sounds but also of representation, whether symbolic or based on some form of abstraction.

In many rituals, for the most part those concerning the survival of the species, requests for protection against plagues or sickness, exorcism, the domination of animals or the elements, as well as the suspension of time, music is the driving force, and may actually constitute the ritual itself.

Hypnosis and trance

One of the properties of instrumental or sung music is that it can make time appear to stand still, lulling the senses of the listener, or literally inducing sleep. That indeed is the principle of the lullaby, whose slow rhythm and repeated words and phrases promote a state of drowsiness.

Subduing animals by means of sound is a common theme in mythology, from Orpheus playing his lyre and attracting

Preceding double page: Shaman in a trance. The Kham Magar people of Nepal learn to play the frame drum as part of a wider initiation process. The shaman's trance is induced not by the music of those around him but by his own use of a drum.

Opposite: Before removing a piece of cedar wood, which is used in the manufacture of a whole variety of different objects, the Kwakiutl Indians address prayers to the spirit inhabiting the tree, entreating mercy and protection. Photograph by Edward S. Curtis.

wild beasts to seat themselves at his feet to Waïnämoïnen, inventor of the harp in Finnish mythology, who created a state of ecstasy in all living things which succumbed to the charms of his music. And then there are the snake-charmers of India and Pakistan, or the tale of the rats drawn to the sound of the pipe and led out of the town of Hamelin to be exterminated by the piper who had bewitched them – and who then led away all the children to the tune of another pipe. Judging by what we learn from mythological tales, medieval legends and fairy stories, it seems that each species is addressed by a different timbre of instrument attuned to its particular sensibility.

The influence of sounds is a common theme in Chinese poetry, and a magical significance attaches to techniques of playing the strings of the zither, manipulations that are modelled on the observations of the attitudes and movements of particular animals. These include, for example, the swimming motion of a fish, the flapping of a bird's wings and the characteristic gait of various quadrupeds. Nature, both animal and vegetable, is the primary source for the gestures the musician is supposed to use when touching the strings. He is meant to absorb these movements by direct observation and concentration, tapping an inbuilt talent for mimicry that is based on a kind of assimilation, a symbiosis of complementary modes of expression.

Gestures based on animals and nature are also central to dance and to the form of Chinese gymnastics called *tai chi*. All such techniques, or pathways, are developed from communion with nature, while maintaining a state of alertness and openness to experience that is rooted in the denial of the self. As body and spirit are liberated, they become receptive to invisible but very real powers, which they are then able, in their turn, to express in a form echoing that of the original.

Attendant spirits

To acquire a playing technique based on animal gestures and behaviour, it is necessary to transform oneself, to cross the threshold that takes the musician or the shaman out of himself and into another dimension of reality that he wishes to represent.

In the past, dances involving the use of masks and disguises sought to imitate animal behaviour in very much the same fashion. In representations of this type, copying animal movements was a means of demonstrating the role played by these creatures in nature, as well as their role vis-à-vis the social group concerned.

To gain the protection of totemic animals regarded as ancestors or allies, man had in effect to become one with the animal species concerned. He would be required to

The magical powers of the *esraj* fiddle appear to have tamed the wild spirit of the peacock that has come to hear the woman play. Detail of an Indian miniature (*Todi Ragini*).

97

Orpheus's lyre

Orpheus charming the animals. Roman mosaic discovered at Blanzy-lès-Fismes (Aisne), 4th century.
Musée Municipal, Laon

Some beings are endowed with the power to create harmony among living beings, both animal and the human. Such beings symbolize within themselves the power of magic and its attributes. Orpheus is a case in point, for by the sound of his lyre he is supposed to have enchanted earthly and supernatural beings, and tamed the animals which flocked to him as though drawn by his person and by the grace of his music. This mythical Thracian bard, sometimes described as the son of king Œagrus and the Muse Calliope, is said to have received from Apollo a lyre with seven strings – seven being the sacred number. He added two more strings, so that each of the nine Muses could be expressed in his music.

Referred to in the *Iliad* and the *Odyssey* under the name *phorminx,* the lyre was originally played with a plectrum of bone or metal, to emphasize the rhythm of ritual dances. The cult of Orpheus is essentially concerned with the freeing of the soul, imprisoned in an earthly body. When Orpheus descended into the Underworld to free his wife Eurydice, who had been killed by a snake-bite, he succeeded in charming the dog Cerberus with his singing, as indeed he was able to charm Hades, and secure the conditional release of Eurydice. Returning to the upper world, however, he looked back too soon towards his wife who was then lost to him forever. Like Hermes, inventor of the lyre, Orpheus provides a link between the human, animal and supernatural worlds, through the magic of his music. Animals, being supremely sensitive to sounds, become his willing slaves. The purpose of the cult of Orpheus is to liberate the soul by the grace of music, acknowledging in doing so the influence that each has on the other.

Above: George Catlin, *The Bull Dance, Mandan O-kee-pa Ceremony*, oil on canvas (detail), c. 1832. The dancers, adopting a stooping posture, wear buffalo skins adorned with leaves that symbolize creation and renewal, and were supposed to ensure the survival of the Mandan Indian people.

Double page overleaf: Dance performed by Amerindians of the Californian coastal region during rituals to promote the fighting spirit of tribal warriors. The initiates wear bear skins, and are possessed, for the duration, of all the real and mystical powers of these animals, in particular their strength and ability to dominate an enemy. Photograph by Edward S. Curtis.

approach certain animals in preparation for the hunt, which became a ritual act in itself, and he would imitate their movements during initiation ceremonies.

Some European sites, dating from 50,000 to 30,000 BC during the Palaeolithic era, contain animal bones and skulls which provide clear evidence of ritual offerings and the existence of magico-religious beliefs that may have included the concept of reincarnation of animals from their bones. It is intriguing to speculate on the possibility of these rituals having been linked to the use of phalanx bones as musical instruments (as discussed in chapter 1), and with the representation of animals on cave walls. According to recent research, the hunters of this period incorporated elements of shamanism into their rituals. Drumsticks have been identified that are similar to those still used by Siberian shamans. Bone drumsticks of a much later date (5th century BC) were discovered on the island of Oleny in the Kara Sea, suggesting that the shamanistic tradition has continued unbroken since Palaeolithic times, most notably in the bear cult prevalent in parts of Asia and North America. Western Europe too provides evidence of shamanism, sculptural representations of guardian spirits having been found at Lascaux. In all these regions, and at all periods in history,

the shaman uses the beating of a drum to enter into a state of trance, he summons attendant spirits, he expresses himself in a secret language and he imitates animal cries, in particular birdsong.

These attendant spirits may appear in the form of familiar animals – among the Siberian and Altaic peoples they are bears, wolves, deer, hares and winged creatures of all kinds – or else in the form of spirits, of the woods, the earth, the mountain or of various plants. The fauna varies according to the region, and with it the spirits that inhabit the landscape, often seven in number. As the shaman imitates the movements and calls of animals, singing, dancing or flying in the manner of his chosen species, he may appear to be possessed, but in fact his transformation of himself into an animal is voluntary and deliberate. Achieved by the wearing of a mask or skin, by mime or the imitation of a cry, this incarnation implies a shedding of humanity, and with it human mortality. The animal represents a direct and tangible link with the afterlife, as animals have fulfilled the role of psychopomp (conductor of souls) since time immemorial: in ancient mythology, it is without exception an animal which conducts men's souls to the place of the dead.

Yü's walk

The practice of wearing feathers to enter another dimension of reality and go up to heaven forms part of ancient Chinese rituals that have survived to the present day – flying being one of the Taoist methods of achieving immortality. Yao and Shun were two of the mythical kings who knew how to 'fly like birds', a power regarded as normal for an individual who was believed to be the physical and spiritual link between heaven and earth. And yet this form of communication between the two spheres, which is made explicit in the myths, was broken off at a certain point in history. Henceforth, it seems, only women were trained in the art, reflecting perhaps the existence of some ancient matriarchy. Even today, in Korea for example, it is usually women who perform the office of shaman.

Yü, who was Shun's successor, has remained famous for his bear dance and 'Yü walk'. This was a shamanistic dance in which the king was transformed by his magical powers into a 'plantigrade' animal, walking flat on the soles of his feet.

The women sorcerers were called *wu*, a Chinese character which suggests a woman with long sleeves dancing between heaven and earth (the homophone of *wu*, meaning 'dance', is of course written differently). Out of the mouth of the *wu* spoke the spirit *shen*, with whom she communed in the course of a trance-induced dance performed with the aid of mime and costume, and to the accompaniment of drums and flutes. The aim of these practices was to establish contact between the living and the dead, to perform cures, to intercede with requests of all kinds, and to regulate power.

There is a close link between these ecstatic dances and animals, and 'Yü's walk' was essentially no different from the dance performed by a shaman. Yü wore a bear skin, and in a certain sense represented the spirit of the animal, in exactly the same way as these customs still survive in shamanic ceremonies in the northern regions of Asia and in North America.

To wear the skin of the animal being hunted was to become that animal, to dance and imitate its behaviour was to establish a relationship with a suprahuman dimension, to copy its breathing and cries was to create a positive empathy. All this had relevance to the purpose of the hunt, conceived as a form of communion and shared experience.

Hunting scene in Mu-lan

Mu-lan IV, The Stag Hunt by Giuseppe Castiglione (Lang Shih-ning; 1688–1766); painting on silk (detail). H. 77 cm (30¼ in.). Musée Guimet, Paris

Giuseppe Castiglione was a Jesuit missionary and painter who went to China in 1714, adopting the Chinese name Lang Shih-ning. A painting by him on four silk scrolls represents the hunt that took place at the autumn equinox in the hills of Mu-lan, today Chengdu. The painting shows the various episodes of this great annual event during which the emperor Qianlong embraced ancient warrior traditions, assuming the role of leader of a Tartar horde, at the head of a veritable army. The scene of encirclement shows the hunt proper, which copies a Mongol battle strategy in which the troops of the Eight Banners rode in a circle 40 kilometres (or 25 miles) in circumference around the imperial yurt, and then closed in, beating the game until it was within the emperor's range. Once the herds of deer were flushed out, one of the beaters would put antlers on his head and don a deerskin; then, blowing the horn called *mu-lan* (meaning 'belling of a stag'), he would copy the animal cry echoing through the woods around him, encouraging the stags to emerge without fear. These hunts were effectively a form of military exercise, renewing the alliance between the lord and his vassals, putting the latter to the test and giving them the chance to prove their valour. For the emperor, the hunt was a magical and religious rite, as well as a political act. It was dedicated to ancestral spirits, to whom the offering of the victims' blood was made. This blood was ritually drunk and shared out among those who had participated in the hunt, demonstrating in this manner their allegiance to their suzerain. Dancing or hunting in animal disguise are features of shamanistic rituals in which hunter and hunted become one, using a common language and sharing a common origin.

Untunn shaman in Siberia, photographed with his drum in 1882. In his role as intermediary between the earthly world and the realm of the spirits, the shaman derives his powers from playing his frame drum, the vehicle by which he enters a state of trance.

106

A great many of the words uttered by the shaman have their origins in the calls of birds and of various animal species. This secret language is indeed sometimes referred to as the 'language of the animals'. In combination with the drumbeat, it is an essential precondition for the successful achievement of the ecstatic state that is the shaman's route into another life-form.

Shaman, sound magician

Communicating with animals via a common language, imitating their calls with whistles, horns and other animal-calls, the transformation into an animal by wearing a mask, fur or feathers or some other attribute, the miming of animal behaviour in a sacred dance – all these represent ways of achieving a condition that, for the duration of the ritual at least, is non-human, and therefore no longer enslaved; rather it belongs to another age, perhaps some mythical past before the fall of a man, a paradisiacal state to which human beings now have access only through magic or ecstatic visions. The shaman rediscovers this lost harmony thanks to music and instruments, in particular the echoing drum.

Even his clothes include acoustic elements, such as the bones that make up the costumes worn by the wandering Tantric monk, or the shamans of the Tungus and Yakuts. Similarly, the Tibetan shaman wears an apron made of bones, while playing a two-sided *damaru* drum made from human skullcaps, and blowing a *rkang-gling* made from a human femur with pierced condyles. Musical instruments of this type reflect the desire common to so many different peoples to identify the vital principle (something that may also have applied to the whistles made of reindeer phalanxes used in the Palaeolithic period). In the Tibetan or Iranian traditions among others, once a human corpse is stripped of flesh and reduced to a skeleton, the bones are considered to be capable of survival, and of resurrection.

Death and resurrection go hand in hand in the bones of the skeleton, human or animal, of which the shaman's costume is composed. During the initiation, the sound of the instruments made of bone is a reminder of the eternal nature of a species, which can be brought back to life at any moment through the evocative magic expressed in the sound produced by the bones. In this context they symbolize the life that was and may be again, because it is in the very material of the bones that the spirit resides.

Frame drum from Lapland. The shaman's instrument *par excellence*, the drum is struck with a bone stick, symbolic of the vital principle, as a means of summoning the spirits, and to accompany various rituals led by the shaman. W. (max.) 71 cm (28 in.).

Wandering Tibetan monk, or *yogi*, who lives as a hermit and recites the holy texts, *gcod*. The equipment of the *yogi* includes the *damaru* drum and the *rkang-gling* made from a human femur.

Rituals and acoustic attributes

Mythical stories about the invention of musical instruments help to reinforce the position they occupy within a particular ritual, as well as lending plausibility to the impact their sounds – whether animal, human or from the natural world – have on listeners.

Here magic is all. Every detail of the process, from start to finish, is subservient to it, from the magic that is involved in the creation of the musical phenomenon in question, to the magic that is created as a result of it. There is no chronology, for this is an area in which reason does not operate. From one end to the other of this seamless and unbroken sequence of events, passing from means to ends, everything that is achieved by technology, everything that is added to the repertoire, remains secondary when compared to the unique magical effect of the musical performance.

Because of the interconnectedness of all the elements of the environment, visible and invisible, these elements can be made to influence one another, and the course of their development can be altered, in the interests of effective action, intercession or communication. That is the effect of the ritual.

In addition, the musical instruments associated with rituals are chosen for their symbolic significance in respect of their history, the legends attaching to them, their form and the materials of which they are made. The sounds they produce utilize different timbres and wavelengths to imitate cries and evoke natural entities and phenomena. They emphasize gestures, accompany dance, and accentuate movements that are themselves symbolic, referring as they do to particular situations or intentions. Here sound is used for its effect of resonance, rather than as music organized in a melodic line. The instrument becomes both a means of communication, possessed of clearly defined powers, and an attribute of the celebrant.

Among the ritual procedures involving the mediation of musical instruments, some are strictly magico-religious, while others have more to do with social organization – although all are in some degree concerned with the good functioning of society.

The *damaru*, instrument of immortality

In India, the drum is associated with the emission of the primordial sound that lies at the origin of the 'manifestation' and rhythms of the universe. The drum in question is the *damaru*, one of the attributes of Shiva, and of Buddhist *dakini* (female demon goddesses). Its rhythms are traditionally connected with the expansion of the *dharma*, and the instrument was referred to by the Buddha himself as the drum of immortality.

The *damaru* is in the form of an hourglass, and thus symbolizes the eternal amd inexorable passage of time, leading ultimately to death, within the cycle of human existence. But it also implies the possibility of a reversal, a return to an original state. Top and bottom are mirrored, and reversal of the drum is necessary for the flow to be maintained. Continuous movement and communication are effected by passage through the bottleneck. Emptiness and fullness follow one another in succession, moving from above to below, from the heavenly to the terrestrial.

In its general shape the *damaru* resembles a calabash, but it is also reminiscent of the alchemist's alembic, consisting of two containers representing the sky and the earth, the bottleneck between them being the site of the actual 'manifestation'. The flow, whether of sand or time, occurs as part of a cyclical process that is at first imperceptible and then speeds up and becomes precipitate. The symbolic significance of Shiva's *damaru* drum is that the two halves of the hourglass are inverted triangles, *linga-yoni*, the central point of contact, the *bindu*, being the origin of the 'manifestation'.

In Tibet, the *damaru* appears most often in the form of the small drum known as the *rnga-chung*, which is made in the form of an hourglass with whirling balls. It can also be a skull drum, *thod-dar* or *thod-rnga*, made of two joined human skullcaps with membranes stretched over the open sides, or it may be larger, made of wood and painted with macabre scenes, and used in the ritual *gcod* or *gcod-dar*.

The sound emitted by the *damaru* is called *shabda* or 'primordial sound'. When associated with the ritual sceptre *rdo-rje/vajra*, the *damaru* embodies the notion of 'fitness of means', *thabs/upaya*, which, in combination with wisdom, *shes/prajna*, is the key to the achievement of enlightenment. The booming sound of the instrument is thought to assist the process.

A number of awesome divinities called 'protectresses of religion' have the *damaru* drum as their attribute, as do other divine beings, who may be heroes or heavenly messengers from the paradise of the Indian Buddhist missionary Padmasambhava, or else religious masters. The drum/attribute is in every case held in the right hand of the figure represented and is associated with other accessories made of bone, such as the trumpet *rkang-gling* or the skull cup *thod-phor*, also the small bell *dril-bu*.

Tibetan iconography shows the *damaru* wielded by the Mgon-po, White Jewel and Master of Life, and their two assistants, also by the tutelary deity 'Khor-lo sdom-pa and the attendant Rdo-rje phag-mo. The guardians of the mandala are similarly equipped, as are other female divinities such as A-phyi and certain of the twelve *bstan-ma*. One of these, mounted on a turquoise lion, holds the drum *cang-te'u* and the pipe *gling-bu*. In *The Secret Visions of the Fifth Dalai-Lama* are featured a number of white *dakini* carrying the *damaru* and small bells. Mandarava, the wife of

Padmasambhava, is shown with the same attributes. Other heroic figures which figure in the monthly ritual dances are equipped in the same way. Padmasambhava himself, in two of his eight manifestations, is shown holding a *damaru* in his right hand, while in the left he holds either a mirror or a skull cup.

Although the instrument also plays a part in Bon religious rituals, it does not figure prominently in the iconography associated with the pantheon of deities belonging to this Tibetan tradition.

Some writers have used detailed descriptions of the parts of the *damaru* drum as the point of departure for the development of theoretical doctrine, using the instrument as sign and reference-point for meditation. Mention is therefore made of the fabric 'belt', decorated with shells,

Tibetan Buddhist monk in Lhasa, holding a *damaru* drum and *dril-bu* bell. The sounds emitted by the *damaru*, and the different elements of which it is composed, all have their place within the symbolic system that is fundamental to Buddhist religious beliefs.

which separates the two elements of the hourglass, of the whirling balls and their percussive action, and of the instrument's fabric carrying-handle, whose decorative elements each have a symbolic significance: the five colours, the trilobate motif, the hook, the mirror, human hair, fragments of tiger or leopard, spherical bells, etc. Each of these elements is celebrated for its form, colour and material, providing the basis for the metaphysical parallels that validate the *damaru*'s role as an object of meditation. In one instance its acoustic qualities are described as an 'encouragement to the yogi to rouse himself and do good to others'.

In ritual usage, the manipulation and playing of the *damaru* must be carried out using precisely ordained gestures. The instrument should never be put down on its end, but positioned so that the male skull (the skin of which is supposed to have been coated with sperm) is to the musician's right, while the female skull (smeared with menstrual blood) is to his left. This arrangement follows the traditional established order of father/mother, right/left, masculine/feminine.

The celebrant holds the instrument by its handle and rotates it with a sharp flick of the wrist, causing the balls to strike the two skins of the drum simultaneously. The exact sounds will differ, depending on the rhythm of the texts, but they are typically described as 'terrible sounds', 'thunderclaps', or a 'crack'. Some texts specify the precise role of each musical instrument, as in the *gcod* ritual, for example:

… a trumpet made from a femur to control genies and demons,
A *damaru* to quell apparitions,
A bell hung with small bells to subdue the *mâtrikâ*....

The *dril-bu*, or wisdom

Foremost among the acoustic attributes of various Buddhas, protective deities and religious masters is the *dril-bu*, a small bell with an internal clapper. The *dril-bu*'s proportions and decorations of lotus petals, monsters' heads etc. correspond to an exact typology and the bell is equipped with a handle 'in the form of a half-*vajra*'. In contrast to the *vajra* which represents thunder and the adamantine world, and which is an attribute of Indra, this small bell represents the world of phenomena and external appearance. The *vajra* ('thunder diamond') sceptre or *rdo-rje* is held in the right hand and symbolizes the means, or *upaya*, necessary to attain a state of knowledge, while the small bell held in the left hand represents wisdom. Everything about these two objects is opposed. They are supposed to represent the duality of phenomena, which it is believed will disappear once they have been joined together in a mystical union when enlightenment is achieved.

Other ritual objects with an acoustic function are the *rkang-gling* and *rkang-dung*, 'pipes made of a man's leg', which is to say fashioned from human femurs. Trumpets of the same shape may be made either of metal or animal horn. Metal horns are often used in pairs, played either in unison or alternating.

Above: In the Indian tradition, the *damaru* drum is associated with the figure of Shiva, Lord of the Dance. In this context, the playing of the *damaru* represents the divine act of Creation. Detail of an Indian miniature.

Opposite: An indispensable instrument of Buddhist ritual, the *dril-bu* bell is always held in the left hand. It is played in short, repeated rhythmic bursts.

Double page overleaf: Detail of a painting on canvas (*thanka*) of the 'Master of cemeteries', showing demons inhabiting the charnel house of the god Sitavarna; each carries a frame drum with a handle, *rnga*.

Instruments as attributes of power

Bronze bell (*gshang*), with flared rim and internal clapper. The decoration of the interior features three concentric circles, symbolizing the three bodies of the *dharma*, and eight engraved motifs in the form of the petals of a lotus opened out into a corolla. Used by priests in the highly specific context of Bon ritual, the *gshang* remains the attribute of those who communicate with the spirits of the dead and possess healing powers. Dolpo valley, Nepal. D. 10 cm (4 in.).

Bronze bell with internal clapper from Benin; pyramidal in form, it is decorated on two of its sides with sculpted features familiar from masks used in local dances. Bells of this type were carried only by the king as attributes of authority. Benin state, Nigeria. H. 14 cm (5½ in.); W. 8 cm (3¼ in.).

Damaru drum with whirling balls; in the shape of an hourglass, it is also called a skull drum when made from human crania. Here the body is made of wood (carved in imitation of two skullcaps) and is decorated overall with paintings of religious scenes. The *damaru* is used in a variety of ceremonies, often in association with the *rkang-gling*. It is normally played inside Tibetan monasteries or by Bon monks. D. 20 cm (7¾ in.).

The *rkang-gling* trumpet, made from a human femur. The mouthpiece section is protected by a metal mount, while the pierced condyles which form the bell are covered in leather studded with turquoises and coral. Often held in one hand, while the other is used to shake the *damaru*, it is the attribute of Buddhist monks and hermits endowed with magic powers, capable of conjuring up hail or trance-induced flight, but its use is chiefly associated with funerary rites. L. 35 cm (13¾ in.).

A Tibetan heaven

The bodhisattva Green Tara, thanka, 18th century.

Musée Guimet, Paris

'Big drums, conches, clay drums, timpani, cymbals and tambourines, floods of
music, all the most melodious sounds in the world, we offer them up to the
most excellent of all incarnations.'

Addressed by the monks, to the sound of the *dril-bu*, to the bodhisattva Tara,
these words serve as a reminder of the musical splendours associated with
the Buddhist heavens. Representations of Tara's heaven show particularly
large numbers of instruments: drums, long trumpets, *sil-snyan* cymbals,
flutes, oboes, and lutes, not forgetting the whirling drum damaru
manipulated by the master of the rituals. Their melody, dominated by the
sound of bells, is said to represent the song of the *kalapingka* bird.

As we see depicted in *thankas*, the music of peace dedicated to Tara is
played within the monasteries. It is this music that gives her life and
substance – as with an icon, the quality of divinity depends on the
worshipper, it is fuelled by offerings and prayers, wishes and incantations
transmitted through music. By its very nature, the musical offering rises
towards the heavens, leaving the world behind. Only through music can
human beings sublimate their condition.

The instruments, musicians and dancers who surround the deity are
indications of this invisible link between music and the divine world, and of
the special role played by sound in communicating with the celestial order.

Many other instruments are introduced into ritual situations of every kind and description – they do not need to be attributes of divinities. These are aerophones such as the telescopic trumpets *dung-chen* and the oboes *rgya-gling*, which are usually played outside monastery walls. The conch *dung-dkar*, the drum *rnga*, the stone chime *rdo-rting*, the gong *'khar-rnga*, or again the *gandi* struck with a mallet, are more instruments of summons, in particular to give the signal for members of a monastic community to assemble.

Yet other instruments, in particular the big drum *rnga* and the cymbals *sbug-chal* or *sil-snyan*, are used to punctuate texts, whether read aloud, sung or chanted. They perform the same regulatory role in the performance of the ritual dance *cham*, being generally responsible for keeping time, whether it be musical tempo, the rhythm of the dance or communal chanting.

The secret alchemy of mortars

In China, when exceptional events such as natural catastrophes threatened the social order, the people would resort to forms of associative magic enacted in ceremonies designed to influence the course of events for the better.

In the case of summer drought, following the ancient tradition according to which utensils such as mortars and furnaces were supposed to produce toads and frogs, a great ritual sacrifice was performed; this involved the setting out of cooking pots on a raised mound and exposing them to the sun, while in the streets ceremonies involving pestles and mortars took place. Animals, notably cockerels and pigs, would be sacrificed to the accompaniment of the beating of drums.

In the age of Confucius (551–471 BC), in the principality of Lu, rain-making ceremonies were performed by men imitating the movements of a dragon in their dancing. The fact that it was men who enacted these rituals is consistent with the importance accorded to the observance of the *yin* (female) or *yang* (male) orientation inherent in all natural phenomena. Since water was already associated with *yin* energy, the presence of women would tend to create an excess of it and could well provoke the opposite effect to the one intended, resulting in floods; women were always kept well away from this type of ritual.

The instrument used to introduce the ritual music *ya* is the mortar, or wooden trough or box; played as a prelude to the action, it is struck with a pestle called *chui*. This was considered the most precious instrument of all, both

Preceding double page: Always played in pairs, the gigantic telescopic trumpets, *dung-chen*, emit a very low frequency of sound. From a vantage point high up on the monastery roof, Tibetan monks use these instruments to send out long, modulated summonses at dawn and dusk, or to greet the arrival of a religious leader.

Left: As they set about their work, Japanese women take advantage of the intrinsic rhythmic potential of pestle and mortar, as well as the changes in the quality of the sound as the consistency of the material changes. *The Dance of Shitateage Ryômen Tamagawa*, print by Kitagawa Utamaro (1753–1806).

Mortars and rain

The connection between 'water' and 'mortars' is reflected in the written form

of the word and in the way it is pronounced, which is the same as for

the word *qiu* used to designate 'hillock' ; the latter character represents

a mound with a concave summit, foreshadowing the shape of the mortar;

originally mortars were no more than holes dug in the ground, as we can see

from the character *qiu* meaning 'mortar'; the sign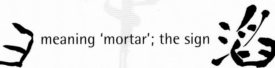

represents a hand on a mortar; when associated with the sign for 'water'

 , it represents 'floods'.

because of its antiquity and on account of the symbolism associated with it, reminiscent as it was of the mulberry tree with all its legendary connotations of the Tree of Life, dwelling of the sun, etc. Its opposite number is the instrument used to close the proceedings, the scraper or tiger-box *yü*. The hollowed-out form of the mortar (which is therefore *yin*), beaten by a pestle (which has *yang* connotations because of its appearance and loud clear sound), has a direct symbolic association with fertility, for the mortar is the vessel in which millet is ground when the pestle is activated.

The scraper, which features a series of wooden teeth, hence *yang* in form, is played with a short brush-like implement which is passed three times over the serrated wood, producing a characteristic low rasping sound that is *yin* in nature.

Coffins, whether of stone or wood, also mimic mortars, because of their shape. Essentially, the mortar is a place in which a mutation occurs, whether this is the journey to the afterlife (or a birth) – given that the form of the mortar is also that of the cradle. It may also be a gestatory object – where *yin* and *yang* couple and are separated, like wheat from the chaff – or the crucible in which a secret alchemy is performed that engenders the cycles of life, and therefore brings about death. The form and function of mortars are similar to those of the wooden drums made out of hollow

tree-trunks that serve as channels between heaven and earth, traversed by the generations.

Hollow tree-trunks, we should remind ourselves, are traditionally viewed both as dwelling places of the sun and as royal drums. A trough made from the wood of the mulberry tree was used in the celebrations of this solar cult, in which the key events were the morning bath taken by the sun, its fight with the ocean and its eventual baptism by water. Numerous minorities in the Chinese-speaking world still use mortars as musical instruments and quite often it is the continuing popularity of the music that has ensured their survival. Several communities in Taiwan – Atayal, Cao and Amei – use a pestle to grind rice or millet during rituals held on the occasion of harvest festivals. The rite takes place inside or outside the house of the village elder. A hole is made in the ground and covered over with a piece of wood, on which the grain is then scattered. This not only represents a return to the original form of the drum, which was a covered ditch, but it also serves to improve the acoustic. A more complex musical effect is achieved by employing the pestles, which in this fertility ritual are wielded exclusively by women, of varying lengths. They may be made of bamboo canes with jar-like extensions at both ends, or consist simply of canes naturally closed at both ends by the nodes in the bamboo stem. Depending on its size, each pestle produces a different note, and the

When bronze drums are suspended from a frame, the intensity of the sound is increased tenfold. Regarded in parts of China as magic weapons, drums of this sort are believed to be capable of frightening the enemy, generating thunder and even starting fires at a distance.

Decoration and symbolism

Formerly an emblem of royal power and agrarian rites, bronze drums tended to lose their role as cultural objects primarily associated with kings and the nobility as private ownership of land became the norm. Drums could be readily sold or exchanged and, once stripped of their sacred significance, they came to represent simply material wealth.

The decoration of these drums nevertheless retains social and ritual connotations: on drums used exclusively for funerary purposes, stylizations of bovine creatures, expressed as skulls or horns, seem to refer to the prowess of warriors or head-hunters. The theme of the star or the sun often recurs, in the middle of the head of the bronze drum, surrounded by concentric circles; other recurring themes are fights with animals, horse races and the stylized battle-axes or daggers associated with head-hunting.

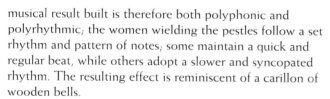

musical result built is therefore both polyphonic and polyrhythmic; the women wielding the pestles follow a set rhythm and pattern of notes; some maintain a quick and regular beat, while others adopt a slower and syncopated rhythm. The resulting effect is reminiscent of a carillon of wooden bells.

In certain circumstances, a mortar fashioned from a block of wood or stone is used as the resonating chamber against which the pestles are pounded. Sometimes the mortar is turned over and the sound is made by the stamping of several women's feet. Georgius Candidius, when he journeyed to Taiwan in the seventeenth century as a missionary of the Dutch Reformed Church, noted in his writings: 'They had turned large mortars upside-down and were dancing on them, which made a lot of noise. Two rows of four or five women were lined up on each of them, backs to back, moving their feet and hands and so forth, each row taking it in turn....'

Bronze drums

Bronze drums feature in the most ancient myths, and are generally associated with warfare, earth and thunder spirits and ancestor spirits.

Such are the vibrations set up by this instrument when it is beaten that it quite transcends its physical reality as a metal vessel and takes on the guise of a living being. When men hear its sound, they mobilize themselves for a common task (as among the Karens and the Burmese) or hold themselves in readiness for war. 'At the sound of the drums

being beaten on the mountain top, the southern barbarians assemble their forces', a Chinese text informs us. Elsewhere it is said that 'when the tribes mean to wage war among themselves, they beat their drums, and then the people mass together like clouds'. The allusion to clouds is anything but fortuitous, emphasizing as it does the link between the sound of drums and thunder. Not only do these instruments serve as a call to arms for the troops, they are also believed to frighten the enemy. Drums carried into battle on the backs of elephants used to perform a similar role.

The function of bronze drums at princely courts is reminiscent of the use made of particular membranophones at the court of the Malayan sultans. The arrival of the sultan was announced by a big drum, and during his absence, two large membranophones or *negara* would act as his symbolic representatives. During banquets and other festivals, an ensemble of eight instruments made up of a combination of drums and horns (*nafiri*) was used to represent the family group headed by a hereditary chief.

If any unauthorized person were to touch these drums, which according to tradition were inhabited by spirits, the offence was punishable by immediate death. Even the guardian of the drum had no personal rights of ownership with regard to the instrument, he served simply as an

Bronze drum, *mohara thuk*, from Thailand. The head is decorated with four frogs, positioned symmetrically. These creatures are said to represent rain, and beating the bronze drum is supposed to bring rainfall. H. 28 cm (11 in.); D. 40 cm (15¾ in.).

Mythical creature with human head and a body composed of parts of various animal and aquatic species. It represents metamorphosis, the theme of many of the legends concerning the origins of musical instruments. Detail of an Indian miniature.

intermediary or spokesman; his was simply the hand that caused the drum to vibrate. Used as an instrument of summons, the bronze drum not only demands prompt attendance, but fosters an abstract sense of community. Quite apart from the sound it produces, it personifies the group, encouraging unity and stimulating a sense of belonging and a sense of duty.

One of the most useful and self-evident functions of the drum was that it could also be used in rain-making ritual, by the simple expedient of being turned upside-down. Furthermore, it could be employed as a magical weapon, capable not only of frightening the enemy with its powerful booming sound, but also of exploiting its capacity to generate thunder.

In the sense that it fosters a spirit of community, sublimated in the person of the chief, it is an 'ornament', similar to a heraldic device, that sums up the essence of a nation and its destiny. Hence, in the case of drums captured from a defeated enemy, it was precisely because of the fact that they personify the social group that they have been so highly prized as trophies and that offerings were made to them at the local temple.

The same function and significance attaches to the wooden Amerindian drums, *teponazli*, regarded as important spoils of war when captured from an enemy, or as national treasures that needed to be preserved for the salvation of the community.

Conquerors and invaders were aware of the totemic, cultural and group significance that some of these instruments possessed, and consequently set about their destruction with as much ferocity as if they were the native peoples themselves. That was certainly true in ancient Peru, which was laid waste in the sixteenth century by the Spanish conquistadors, where the *teponazli* were the most jealously guarded of treasures. It was also the case in parts of black Africa where Western colonialists, Christian missionaries and Muslim rulers, when confronted with the bloody rituals associated with these drums, embarked on the systematic destruction of these instruments. In all these cases, what was at stake was the very soul of a people, the cult of its ancestors and its foundation legends, which were shored up by a form of magic which ensured that, at least for the duration of a ritual, historical time was suspended, and its mythic status restored.

The metamorphosis and personification of instruments

In legends, the origin of musical instruments is often attributed to a metamorphosis, usually from the animal state (the animal will usually be mythical, or an entity of intermediate nature, halfway between man and beast), before materialization as a musical instrument. These objects are to be regarded as repositories of spirits and supernatural forces, dwelling places they have chosen to occupy for a short time. The same would therefore be as true of instruments as it would in respect of the human body, which is inhabited by the soul until a new metamorphosis occurs. Sometimes the instrument will actually enshrine the living spirit of an individual, so that the destruction of the one leads to the death of the other. The simple fact of losing an instrument implies a mutation both in the owner's life and in the nature of the instrument.

Sometimes instruments are found by chance, and then they are like signs or pledges of power. If they then disappear, the 'heavenly mandate' of which they were the guarantee disappears with them. In that respect they resemble bronze vases, lithophones, images of the world and magic squares, possession of which is a guarantee of permanent protection, and a mark of temporal power.

Legend has it that, in the course of his voyages, the king Mu lost the Spirit Drum *linggu*, which was transformed into a yellow snake. The king then planted a pawlonia, a tree whose wood is used to carve war drums and zithers. This Spirit Drum is described as a triple drum with six faces, representing the earth spirits, and it is to be distinguished from the drum with eight faces called the Thunder Drum, which is used by heavenly spirits, and the drum with four faces that is reserved for ancestor worship.

By virtue of its sacred properties, a drum has a distinct personality, which may be that of the spirit of the community, or may represent ancestral souls. For this reason it sometimes bears a name as if it were an individual. The naming of bronze drums in parts of south-east Asia reflects their sacred character, in the eyes of their makers and those who use them. In the Moluccas, they are called 'moon', in the case of a large drum with a particularly imposing face, or 'thunder-drum' (*tifa-guntur*), or elsewhere they may be treated as a person, with a name such as *Bo so napi* ('old mother') or *chu-ko*, a name common in southern China that alludes to the famous general Zhu Geliang (181–243). In Sumbawa (Indonesia), for example, drums are given the names of people, such as Makalamau, Waisarinci or Saritasangi. Elsewhere they may simply be designated 'large vessel' (*sanggu* or *tempayan*), as in the case of drums preserved in the Museum Nasional in Jakarta.

Often the name given to an instrument is kept secret. Because of this taboo, the name must never be mentioned in ordinary circumstances. Sometimes the drum has to be fed, as by spreading rice, cereal grains, blood or feathers on its surface, the purpose being to reinforce its magical powers. On the occasion of the inauguration of a drum, pigs and hens are sacrificed in order to impart, through the blood of these animals, vital energy to the instrument.

A drum that has been sanctified, personalized and revered in this way can truly be said to be inhabited by a spirit. Such a spirit may appear to any thief who attempts to steal the instrument; he would then be pursued by visions of the being incarnate in the drum, which may manifest itself, for example, in the form of a tiger.

Drum and concubine

A drum of this type is a tangible symbol of the chief's supremacy, in just the same way as the vertically or horizontally positioned wooden drums that feature in solar cults associated with the mulberry tree. Possession of a drum and the size of the instrument are indicators of the social status of the owner. Thus, peasants may have small wooden drums, while village elders may own much larger ones that hang ostentatiously outside their houses. Such drums are in a certain sense the 'concubines' of the chief, with whom he has relations of a sexual nature.

While the intimate relationship that exists between the chief and his drum in some sense resembles that of a married couple, it is equally that of a warrior and his magic weapon. At the same time, the community as a whole reveres the instrument as the repository or personification of the collective spirit.

The relationship is therefore dual in character: the drum symbolizes the close, magical ties by which it is bound to

Symbols of social status, the timpani *nagara* and *tyanko* are suspended from the roof of a lean-to extension outside the musician's house in Nepal.

The wooden barrel on which the bronze drum and its drumstick rest may also be used as an extension of the body of the drum when it is suspended vertically, the purpose being to modulate the sound. Miao people, Guizhou province, China.

the chief, while the link with the community is of a social nature. The two forms of relationship are indivisible.

In Tibesti, a mountainous area of northern Chad, the drums *kwelli* and *nang'ara* are normally struck only by men from the highest caste in the social hierarchy. There are strict rules to be observed: first, the right to play them is restricted to men, and prohibited to women and uncircumcized boys; second, only the chief can use the *kwelli*, which he employs to communicate information, both within the village and while travelling.

The *nang'ara* is made especially for the investiture of a new head man (*derde*). Only when the newly installed chief beats this drum does his power becomes effective. It is also used when a judgment has been issued, the drumbeat giving the pronouncement the force of law. It can solemnize words, but it cannot produce anything resembling intelligible language: that is the task of stringed instruments capable of sustaining melody.

Instruments and funerary practices

There are Chinese texts in existence that describe the very ancient custom of burying a drum alongside its owner or the person it represents, usually a chieftain. This was common practice among the non-Chinese Man people and the southern barbarians. Many prototypes have been recovered *in situ*, mostly full-size but including some miniatures. These are decorated in a variety of ways, often with sculptures of frogs. In Java, certain instruments of this type dating from the eighteenth century were buried in cemeteries and in places reserved for the remains of dead chieftains.

Sometimes these drums were inverted and filled with coins or cowries – the small shells formerly used as currency. In other places, gongs were used as offerings for the dead; the Moi people of North Vietnam regarded these instruments as necessary attributes for the chief, who was enabled by this means to command his men even from beyond the grave.

The fact of burying an instrument, particularly a drum, implied a considerable financial loss both for the dead man's family and for the community at large, while at the same time it deprived them of an object possessed of magical powers. Later the practice of burying drums with the body of the deceased was abandoned and miniature versions were substituted, or fragments taken from the original would be used, perhaps a carved elephant or other decoration capable of representing it symbolically.

In Burma, the practice of burying a bronze drum with its owner was discontinued in the sixteenth century under the great conqueror Bayinnaung (1550–81) of the Taungu dynasty. Instead parts of the drum were removed, such as the frog sculptures, and these were placed in the tomb. Numerous miniature drums have been exhumed at many different sites; these are comparable to specimens made of clay or paper – which in China are called *mingqi* – of the type used to accompany the dead in many civilizations. Nevertheless, it is true that in some tombs, notably in North Vietnam, miniatures of this description have been found alongside the real thing. Several of these buried bronze drums show evidence of holes where a piece of metal has been removed. The justification for this was that by so doing the members of the community could ensure that the *K'la* spirits inhabiting the drum would remain with them, so that they could still legitimately regard themselves as the possessors of a drum.

Other more radical operations include the 'killing' of the drum, before placing it in the tomb, so that the instrument can be seen to have been destroyed. In the case of drums recovered from Shizhaishan, an ancient cemetery site in Yunnan province, the very heart of the instrument – the star in the centre of the playing surface – has been removed, and even in some instances the complete surface.

Recent ethnological investigations have shown the existence of the funerary practice that consists, on the occasion of the death of a chieftain, 'in laying his body on a row of drums, while one of his drums is sacrificed by being perforated, so rendering it unusable' (Sorensen), in other words reducing it to the same condition as the lifeless body, and making it ready for entry into a new world.

The ancestral voice

The sound the drum emits is often thought to be the voice of dead souls, especially of founding members of a tribe. In that respect we can therefore compare the function of the bronze drum to that of the bull-roarer, which in other parts of the world is said to reproduce ancestral voices when used in sacred rites. The unearthly sound that emanates from it is also said to be a means of recalling dead souls to their dwelling place: harmonious sound is meant to have a soothing effect on the dead, whether ancestors or not.

The bronze drum, like its wooden counterpart, is designed to be used in a variety of circumstances, but as we have seen, it plays a considerable role in matters concerning magic and the afterlife. These instruments are thought to be the dwelling places of ancestors or great figures from the past, and are believed to contain their voices within them. Drums in south-east Asia are frequently associated with historical figures such as the Chinese generals Ma Yuan and Zhu Geliang.

Annual sacrifices, in the form of offerings of rice and drink set aside from the domestic food supply, are made to such drums in ceremonies accompanied by festivities and dancing. Studies have shown that the decorations on the main body of instrument represent detailed and precise illustrations of these practices.

The respect and fear inspired by bronze drums must have had implications for their safekeeping. Perhaps this explains why so many have been found high up on hill tops or mountains, or even more frequently on volcanoes. According to tradition, they have fallen from the sky, but in most cases the native peoples would have placed them in spots specifically indicated for Thunder Drums. Other popular hiding places were in the woods, in a pool beside a tree, in a hollow tree, or in a temple or a prince's residence, as is the case in Bali, where possession of such a drum adds to the ruler's prestige and is considered to confer a magical protection on the population.

Silence and intimations of music

The *qin* subsumes within itself the harmony of all sounds, so what is the point of struggling to make it heard aloud?', speculated Tao Yuan-ming. Often ritual function is more important than exploitation of the musical properties of the instrument: it may have musical capabilities, but does not give expression to them. It is precisely these faculties of silence, these intimations of music that are relevant in the case of the Chinese zither *guqin*, which is appreciated more for its symbolic significance than for any musical pleasure to be obtained from its silken strings, the sound of which is barely audible when used in the playing of ritual music. The instrument is included in the ensemble simply by virtue of being the representative of one of the fundamental categories. When the *guqin* is played elsewhere, it will be in very restricted circles, being used only where it can be clearly heard.

In Rwanda, there are certain dynastic drums (*ingabe*) which serve only as symbols of royal power and are never played. That situation is partially echoed in the royal rituals held in Benin, where a ballet is performed in honour of the

Musician playing the Korean twelve-stringed zither *kayagum*, which has silk strings and twelve adjustable bridges. The instrument is capable of generating a variety of sound effects, including a broad vibrato and modulations of pitch.

127

Images of the *ajogan* dance, the fifth of a suite of six dances performed at court during the reign of king Gbefa (1948–76) in Porto-Novo, Benin. The *alunlun* are used first as sticks and then as sistra or scrapers. With their right hands, the women push metal rings up to the top of the sticks and then let them fall. The rings make a chinking sound as they slide down against the grooved surface.

king of Porto-Novo. The dances bear the names of various types of instruments, such as 'Our Mother the Thunder is fallen' or 'Male Bell', depending on which drum or bell is used for the musical accompaniment. The seven female musicians are the king's wives (seven being the woman's number) who, with the four dancers (corresponding to the four cardinal points of the compass), perform a choreographed sequence that is half-danced and half-walked. The dancers are equipped with instruments that are also attributes associated with the four cardinal points, which they salute when defining the sacred area in which the dance is to be performed.

Before use, the four drums, each made from a wooden cylinder of a different size and having a single membrane, are freshly decorated with paintings in the colours of the python Dangbe, a divinity of the Houeda connected with royalty. The drums symbolize the four corners of the world over which the king rules, and each has a distinctive name. Apart from *Mino Zoje* ('Our Mother the Thunder has fallen'), mentioned above, there are *Ayakpa* ('Zither'), *Dogla* ('Take courage') and *Handun* ('Singing drum').

Of these, only *Mino Zoje* is played with the bare hands, accompanying seven iron bells called *gansu* ('Male Bell'). Other instruments are incorporated in the ritual: the four large calabashes (*gogbo*), instruments used in the dance called *gobun* ('calabash drum'), the sides of which are beaten with the bare hands; rattles called *asan*; wooden rods (*agida*) used to strike the bells, and rods called *hando* ('for singing'), which have no musical function. That is also true of the raft-shaped zithers called *ayakpa*, which the dancers hold but do not play. Other members of the orchestra which are included as reminders of the past, but not played, are the percussion instruments (*livi*) made from earthenware jars, originally designed to be struck on their open top with a leather fan, *afafa*.

In the performance of this suite of ballets, aa special rod (*alunlun*) surmounted by a sculpted bird, is wielded by each of the four dancers as they enact certain choreographed sequences; these rods form part of the ensemble called *ajogan*, which also includes the seven iron bells.

The ballet of the *alunlun*

An engraving of 1730 published in *Le Voyage du Chevalier Des Marchais* shows iron *alunlun* with copper handles, one of them in the shape of a cockerel. The accompanying text describes the instrument as beng 'screwed together and covered with copper rings, with a copper cockerel at the end, used for the King's music'. These rods had a function similar to that of rhythm sticks, making sounds either like a scraper, when slid along the length of the uneven stem, or like a sistrum, when the loose rings tinkled as the dancers beat time on the ground. They were also used as sticks for leaning on. The musical ensemble *ajogan* ('rogue iron') takes its name from this archaic musical instrument, described as a 'rod with sliding rings'.

At the time of the foundation of the town later called Porto-Novo by the Portuguese, sticks made in a similar fashion were planted in the ground as markers to designate the chosen spot. In this context, they functioned like an

axis, indicating a central point from which a new social space would develop. They also functioned as gnomons, being fixed vertically in the ground, marking an event that served as a historical point of departure in time, while simultaneously indicating the daily cycle through the movement of the shadow cast by the sun. Pounding the ground with these *alunlun* is therefore both a repetition of the historical act of foundation, and a means of beating the rhythm of the ritual dance that inaugurates a sacred period. The use of these musical instruments is highly significant as they represent a tradition that goes right back to the great founding father, while the whole dance retraces the legendary epic of the foundation myth.

The forge myth

The blacksmith is an indispensable member of the social group. He forges the agricultural implements necessary for survival, weapons for the group's self-defence, and ritual objects used by the community. Everywhere he is feared, because of his association with fire and metals: the latter taken from mother earth and charged with an energy that needs to be mastered; the former needing to be tamed and kept under tight control. Having such power over the elements gives him a position of dominance and a mysterious authority. Identified as he is with the forces he manipulates, the blacksmith is an ambivalent figure who acts as mediator between the living and the dead. In Tibesti, northern Chad, the fabrication and playing of the drum known as *kidi* are associated with the blacksmith, being used to accompany his songs. This drum is one of the more visible indications of his social status, and no one outside his caste is allowed access to it. The blacksmith's position in society is also expressed in the words of songs – public hymns of praise addressed to him – which are performed to the accompaniment of the beating of a drum; here an oral tradition is closely identified with the operations of the social hierarchy.

The king De Tofa, who ruled Porto-Novo from 1874 onwards, left a carillon of seven bells, four of which were cast in white metal – nickel silver – and not forged. These produced a purer, more prolonged and more crystalline sound than traditional iron bells, and their exceptional quality lent the palace *ajogan* a unique status. No other princely household or minister possessed anything that could be considered remotely comparable.

Thus a particular sound, resulting from a particular manufacturing technique, becomes in effect a part of the personality of the group which the instrument represents, as personified by the chief, subsuming within it everything from the historical genesis of the casting of these bells to the symbolic meaning attached to them by their owners or by the neighbouring tribes.

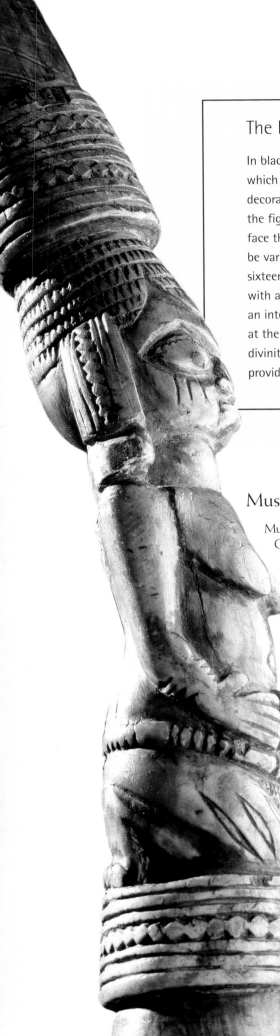

The Ifa ritual

In black Africa, certain bells are used in conjunction with a round tray for a method of divination called *ifa*, which is the means by which the Yoruba gods are enabled to help those who invoke their assistance. In the

decorative frieze around the edge of the tray appears the figure of Eshu, the messenger god, which should face the soothsayer, even though the other motifs may be varied. The soothsayer interprets the position of sixteen nuts thrown onto the tray, which is covered with a thin layer of sawdust. The carved ivory bell has an internal clapper; it is shaken and struck and aimed at the tray in order to attract the attention of the divinity presiding over the ceremony and interceding to provide inspiration to the soothsayer.

Musical divination

Musical divination goes back at least to ancient Greece, where the priests and priestesses would often deliver the god's response in musical form. The oracle of Dodona had to be interpreted through the tinkling of fine metal chains cast into a vessel, or the clashing of bronze cymbals as they moved in the wind.

Among the instruments used for the purposes of divination are the rattle, in black Africa and in Brazil among the Tupinamba Indians (the latter being a rattle with the power of speech, or possessed at least of the voice of the spirit inhabiting it), and iron bells struck with a hammer, used in association with a mask during ceremonies of the Do cult.

Another use of musical divination, typically Chinese, is the assessment of the fighting spirit of an adversary by observation of his *qi*. This type of energy manifests itself both as colour and sound, in accordance with the theory of correspondences between the elements, as well as the notion of the *yin/yang* duality. The musical notes are divided into two groups of six that comprise six *yin* pitches and six *yang*, and these are channelled into acoustic tubes called *guan*, where they are measured. Both the quantity and

density of sound can be read off visually according to a system of corresponding colours. Some sources mention only four tubes, but the use made of them is the same, the purpose being divination and the prediction of the outcome of a battle.

The diagnosis offered by the master of music to the Qin officials in this case was actually very similar to the judgment formed by a shaman, for he would predict the outcome of the fighting by 'sniffing the wind' captured in his acoustic tubes facing in the direction of the enemy, Chu, declaring: 'The sound [that comes from this direction] is weak and foretells a great massacre; the kingdom of Chu will proceed inexorably to its defeat.'

The fact that the existence of this divinatory practice in China has been confirmed by historians does of course have implications above and beyond it being linked to divination practices observed in the shamanism of many other peoples. For a start, it forms an integral part of a highly particular and coherent philosophical system relevant to many other areas of Chinese scientific theory, of which it is merely a sideshoot – it could for example equally well be called 'the strategic divination by sounds, illustrating the theory of the duality of energy'.

Warding off demons and summoning spirits

Since ancient times it has been widely believed that the metallic sounds emitted by large and small bells, gongs and cymbals – all the different timbres of jangling, clashing, pealing and tinkling – are capable of putting demons and evil spirits to flight. During a rite of exorcism, the officiating priest carries a small bell. Similar bells are sewn to his vestments so as to ring with every movement he makes, thus protecting him by their constant tinkling. Ceremonies for the casting out of demons, plagues and sicknesses are universal, being performed on fixed dates, as for example during the hurly-burly of Carnival, or else on occasions specifically designated for the protection of individuals or the community. That is the case among the Dusun in Borneo, where the chasing out of demons is performed once a year in a solemn ceremony involving gongs, bells and bronze drums.

Such customs are universal, whatever the specific nature of the local religious practices. They even form the basis of God's commandment to Moses (Exodus, XXVIII 33–4) concerning priestly robes to be adorned with small golden bells, and have been the source of inspiration for the religious accessories used on every continent and at every period, including rattling censers once wielded by Mexican priests. Metallic sounds are not, however, the only remedy; in Rome small clay bells are still rung annually on 24 June – the Feast of St John the Baptist, which coincides with the pagan Midsummer Day when this was the method adopted to drive away witches.

In Tibet, the new year is greeted with a cacophony of metal instruments – bells and cymbals – as well as small *damaru* drums and conches. In Malaysia, the wake for the dead is accompanied by the beating of gongs to keep malicious spirits at bay, a practice that was also customary in ancient Greece. Small bells and spherical bells are for the same reason universally present in Egyptian tombs and on mummies' wrappings. And there are numerous monasteries and tombs, anywhere from ancient Rome to the Far East, with wind chimes suspended above the porch to act as a form of protection.

Opposite: Ivory bell used for divination among the Yoruba people of Nigeria in the first half of the 20th century. The low-relief sculpture of a woman about to give birth is a symbol of fecundity, and therefore of wealth.

Below: Buddhist monastery in Lhasa, Tibet. Numerous small bells are suspended from the eaves of monastery roofs. Clappers are replaced by very thin metallic strips, which are set in motion by the least puff of wind.

In Malaysia, the representation in miniature of an orchestra of gongs and cymbals, placed on a tomb, is enough to drive away evil spirits. In India, once again as a defence against evil influences, 'at the winter solstice (Mahâvrata), people beat the drum and made a din to frighten the black demons that become more dangerous in the season of the long nights. At funerals people break pots; at exorcisms they strike a gong' (Oldenberg). Among the Thonga, a Bantu tribe of east Africa, exorcisms are accompanied by the beating of drums and the shaking of rattles around the person who is possessed, making a deafening racket.

Firecrackers are used not only to get rid of mischievous spirits but also to attract the attention of the gods to offerings being presented to them. They are also a way of summoning the gods. In Japan, a prayer in front of a tomb or an altar is always preceded by a ritual clapping of the hands to summon the *kamis*. Pierre Loti described this practice in *Madame Chrysanthème*: 'From time to time, when the weary spirits were no longer listening, it was accompanied by sharp claps of the hands, or else by the high-pitched sounds of some wooden clapper made of two discs of mandrake root.'

Curing sickness and praying for fertility

The metallic sounds made by certain instruments also have the power to keep sickness at bay. In rituals of this type, silence is observed, so that the spirits make no mistake about the invitation issued to them. In Annam, during a cholera epidemic, all unnecessary noise is forbidden so that only the cholera spirits will respond to the summons and assemble at the site of the cult ceremony; they will thus not be misled into thinking that the ceremony is a festival at which they would inevitably spread the sickness. In Mali, iron bells are paraded through the village during collective rites of protection and beaten regularly by initiates with the aid of sticks or acoustic rings, the purpose being to warn the uninitiated of the passing of the ritual procession and allow them time to get out of the way.

In cases of fever, some Arab peoples attach all sorts of pendants to a sick person's body. Here once again the role of purification and protection is played by objects designed to make sounds, whether hung on garments or suspended in the vicinity of the patient.

There are many peoples who use the playing of idiophones as the equivalent of a protective spell in ceremonies connected with fertility, ranging from conception and birth to the initiation rituals held at the age of puberty.

The wearing of bells and small spherical bells is said to protect the health and fertility of domestic animals of well as of human beings, since stables as well as churches are thought to be haunted by evil spirits and need to be safeguarded in a similar way. In Mongolia, strings of small objects are hung round the necks of camels, producing the same tinkling sound as a cowbell, or sometimes a long bell with a wooden clapper is used.

The bell, symbol of power

Recognized as being, of all musical instruments, the one with the most resonant and penetrating sound, the bell has been adopted as the preferred instrument for marking a rhythm among many African peoples. Capable of executing varied and complex rhythmic sequences, maintaining the beat for singing as well as drumming and dancing, its voice rises above all the other instruments, just as a king rules over his subject peoples.

As well as symbolizing dominance of sound and representing the voice of authority, the bell possesses other attributes associated with the nature of kingship, being designated 'custodian of the voice', 'custodian of iron', and 'custodian of cowrie shells'. It is handled exclusively by the king and, although it remains a musical instrument, it is above all an attribute and emblem of power. That is especially true, for example, in the case of the double iron bell, the *ganviawene* ('bell with two children') – also known as *gankpanwi* ('bell carrying

Preceding double page: The vibrant clashing of the cymbals *shug-chal* (left) is the perfect form of divine musical offering, as made by Buddhist monks in Tibet. The sound waves emitted by Chinese temple bells in Shaanxi province (right) are prayers addressed to the Bodhisattva, a divine figure intermediate between mankind and the enlightenment of Buddha.

Right: Dôtaku bell made in Japan in the Yayoi period (250 BC–AD 250). More than three hundred such bells have been found on the western side of Honshu island. It seems their function was largely ritual and/or symbolic, and they were rarely used for musical purposes.

Opposite: Ringing the long metal bell used by the Dogon of Mali. During funerary rites, different sizes of bells of this type are played in an ensemble. When played in conjunction with other instruments, they have the power to help the soul of the deceased depart from the village, never to return.

its child on its back'), *gansudaside* ('male and female bell') or *abwangan* ('war bell') – which is used as the accompaniment for a magical incantation pronounced every morning by the king when he rises. This is known as the 'king's awakening'. Holding the bell upside-down in his left hand, with the handle pointing downwards, the king raises the open end to his mouth and exhales into the bell, with two long deep breaths. In this mouth-to-mouth communion, a fusion with the instrument is effected by the mediation of his breath. After this the king, punctuating his words with violent blows on the two parts of the bell, pronounces the following incantation in a loud voice:

> The drum fades, the voice of the bell never fades,
> [repeat]
> My voice is there above the Adja, the Ayo, above the Houassa, above
> the Kembeli, above the Gbanbla,
> My voice is there, above them all,
> The drum fades, the voice of the bell never fades,
> My voice is there....

The ringing of the bell becomes mingled with the words uttered by the speaker, which constantly emphasize throughout the incantation the transference operating between the two participants, the one finding expression in the voice of the other: the king's voice is the voice of the bell; and through the bell he communicates with and rules over the surrounding peoples. By identifying himself with the bell, the king believes he also acquires its virtues, the infallibility of its metallic essence and, by association, the quality of a ruler whose authority is universally acknowledged by his people.

This example expresses all the symbolic attributes associated with the sound of the bell, which is used initially to mark the royal accession and then repeated each morning when the king awakens. It is a sound synonymous with the substance of the object, a sound that becomes one with the voice of the king, the collaboration between them serving as a pledge of firm government. The elaboration of these sounds in musical form in the incantation – involving notes of different pitch, rhythm, words, scansion – lends the ritual its magical power.

The fact is, however, that many African bells are not first and foremost instruments for the creation of resonant sound, but above all symbols of authority and power, used to invoke the king's ancestors. At the time of his own investiture, each chief or king has a bell made for his son, thus symbolizing the continuity of sovereign and military power. The bell will either be cast in bronze or sculpted in wood. This emphasis on the succession of the son explains why childbirth occurs so often as a feature of the decoration and sculptural relief found on instruments of this type.

4　　Instruments in Society

And men united in music

The chiming clock follows in a long tradition of time-reckoning instruments that embraces the clepsydra trickling out the hours on the Tower of the Winds in Athens, the Egyptian water-clock and the weight-driven timepieces of the Arab world and the medieval Cistercian monastery. From the days of the horizontal balance to the modern balance wheel, the bell has been our preferred method of signalling the divisions of solar time. At regular intervals throughout that day, its sound is heard ringing out from church towers and public buildings.

The language of bells

The bell fulfils the role of a voice capable of carrying farther than words or shouts, in conveying summonses, warnings or messages that signal the passage of time. It is endowed with all the authority of an intermediary in the regulation of everyday life, and in this respect it resembles the slit drum made of wood, which too has functions of summons and the imposing of order in society.

As well as signalling the time of day, the bell has many other traditional functions: it marks special occasions like annual festivals, and from time to time there will be other distinctive announcements, such as sounding the curfew and in troubled times the tocsin to raise the alarm, tolling the knell, ringing a full peal on joyous or special occasions, summoning the faithful to worship or announcing the daily offices in a monastic order.

Bells have many different voices and registers, and their tone changes according to their role. In relaying messages their sound may be amplified, as in an invitation to attend a gathering, or muted as in a summons to meditation or prayer, or they may announce the hours in a neutral tone. There are as many different types of sounds as there are

roles. In the case of ringing by hand, technically 'ringing' is said to take place only if the bell is swung through nearly a full circle with its mouth uppermost; a bell is 'chimed' if it is swung mouth downwards and struck by the clapper once only with each pull on the rope; if a large bell is suspended at ground level, it is struck by an external hammer.

A whole specialized vocabulary exists on the subject of bell-ringing, reflecting the variety of techniques involved: the language of campanology has grown up around the use of an instrument conceived of as an extension of the human voice and developed, in full consciousness of that fact, as a means of communication.

Mediator and protector, the bell alone fulfils all these varied roles associated with communication, intercession, defence and warning. A multifunctional instrument, it is representative of the whole of society, both in respect of the materials of which it is made and of the symbolism attaching to it; it is an affirmation of life and provides living proof of man's ability to transcend matter.

The instruments of an immutable world

In China, the musical instruments of the ritual orchestra were classified according to their relationship to a symbolic system comprising all the elements of the natural order, so that their pitch and timbre, as well as the materials of which they were made, were at every moment situated within the space-time continuum. On the correlation between these two principles depended the equilibrium of human existence between heaven and earth, and Chinese society was therefore organized so as to ensure strict observance of the rhythms and manifestations of the universe, within a precise ritual developed in the course of a long hierarchical tradition.

Preceding double page: Itinerant musician carrying his *tandura* lute, in Gujarat (India).

Opposite: Peal of bells in Tbilisi in Georgia. The bells ring out over the city at regular intervals, announcing the time of day and providing an accompaniment to prescribed events.

The division of time in China

In China, the bell alternated with the drum to announce the hours and watches, each occupying its own tower to either side of the entrance to the citadel. Time was divided into twelve segments, each representing two hours, based on a system of animal symbolism corresponding to a duodenary cycle and reflecting the daily waxing and waning of *yin* and *yang*.

First hour (from 11 p.m. to 1 a.m.): Hour of the Rat, secretive and furtive, deeply *yin*.

Second hour (from 1 a.m. to 3 a.m.): Hour of the Buffalo, calm and full of vitality.

Third hour (from 3 a.m. to 5 a.m.): Hour of the Tiger, powerful and concentrated.

Fourth hour: (from 5 a.m. to 7 a.m.): Hour of the Hare, alert and active.

Fifth hour (from 7 a.m. to 9 a.m.): Hour of the Dragon of the Eastern Sun.

Sixth hour (from 9 a.m. to 11 a.m.): Hour of the Snake, which proceeds with ease and skill.

Seventh hour (from 11 a.m. to 1 p.m. – midday): Hour of the Horse, dynamic, the apogee of *yang*.

Eighth hour (from 1 p.m. to 3 p.m.): Hour of the Sheep, calm and energetic.

Ninth hour (from 3 p.m. to 5 p.m.): Hour of the Monkey, busy and restless.

Tenth hour (from 5 p.m. to 7 p.m.): Hour of the Cock, marking the waning of *yang*.

Eleventh hour (from 7 p.m. to 9 p.m.): Hour of the Dog.

Twelfth hour (9 p.m. to 11 p.m.): Hour of the Pig.

Thus, the division of time echoes the manifestations of nature, which are personified here, in a manner of speaking, by the attitudes of animals. The twelve animals of the Chinese zodiac are representative both of the animal kingdom and of the human race, because human beings are supposed to be associated from birth with one or other of these prototypes, as can be seen both from their looks and from their behaviour.

At every double hour of the day, man submits to the influence of the dominant animals and moves gradually between *yin* and *yang*, as the sun does, to the regular rhythm of the drum and the bell, whose sounds serve to signal the transition from one period to the next.

In the Chinese world, bells represent among other things the cohesion of the social group. Closely associated with ancestor worship, they would be played, in company with other instruments, in orchestras; evidence of these has been discovered in recent decades in the course of archaeological excavations, revealing that wind, stringed and percussion instruments were used to accompany ritual singing and dancing. These activities would take place at banquets where a family group would gather to summon the spirits of their ancestors by the playing of various instruments. Bells and drums signalled the different phases of the rite, and the sound of bells in concert with other instruments acted as an invitation to the ancestral spirits to appear, to speak their message through the oracle or medium and to confer blessings and benedictions.

Bells, sometimes single examples but more often in sets, have been found only in the tombs of aristocrats, heads of families or regional potentates. From this one may deduce that the simple fact of possessing them implied an elevated social position, if only on account of their intrinsic value. Over and above the privilege enjoyed by their owner the possession of bells apparently implied a duty, if not an obligation, for the head of the family to seek the intercession of ancestors by organizing ritual concerts.

The Temple of the Heavenly Summit, Meishan, Sichuan province, China. Climatic change marks the passage of the seasons and the annual cycle of the religious calendar, whose important festivals are often announced by the ringing of bells.

141

In its own way therefore, within the confines of specific seasonal rituals, the bell was as much a link between heaven and earth as, on another level, was the concept of the king as Son of Heaven, whose influence extended to the whole of the kingdom or Empire.

During the Warring States Period (403–221 BC), the rituals themselves were the object of much dispute. Each petty kingdom or 'state' was vying with the rest for overall control of the State and so would attempt to take upon itself the prerogatives of the sovereign and adopt his ritual practices and functions as its own.

The 'Yellow Bell'

The virtue *de*, which is mentioned in Chinese texts, is the characteristic quality of a ruler that enables him to exercise his authority. It is by means of the emblems that represent him and his ability to personify them, while contenting himself with being no more than a vehicle or instrument, that he fulfils his heavenly mandate (*tianming*). His virtue thus represents his capacity to symbolize, embody, sum up and represent a nation, or in other words to exercise sovereign power. It is by these criteria that his ability as a ruler will be judged. Therefore, what the emperor embodies and represents can and should be measured, for on it depends the order of the world.

Thus, the weights and measures used during his reign will be codified according to an overriding central principle which serves as the standard for all other values that need to be fixed. This central principle is manifested in the fundamental musical pitch *huangzhong*, or Yellow Bell, on

which was based an untempered scale of twelve semitones (*lü*); the *huangzhong* stands for the concept of order as personified by the sovereign.

According to the Zhou dynasty ritual, the calibration of musical pitch corresponds to the content of pipes, acoustic tubes or hollow reeds of varying lengths. The *huangzhong* was determined by the longest bamboo pipe, which was the standard unit of both length and volume, its capacity being the equivalent of roughly one thousand two hundred average-sized grains of millet. In Chinese the word for 'bell', *zhong*, is the homophone of *zhong* meaning 'centre', although the two terms are distinguished graphically. As for *huang*, yellow, it is the colour of the centre, according to the colour system of the magic square, *mingtang*, a microcosm the circumambulation of which by the Son of Heaven in accordance with the seasons determined the divisions of time and the ordering of the empire.

The sovereign occupies the centre. All inward impulses are channelled by him and made to spread outwards to the periphery before returning to the centre. Exactly the same principle applies to the overall administrative organization of the country. The standard that prevails at the centre of power is thus extended to the surrounding areas which are subject to it and owe it allegiance.

Thus, ancestor worship signals the recognition of a common stock, and the desire to address the same guardian spirits. Simultaneously, the bell sounded in the course of these rituals functions as a symbol of unity and shared reverence for particular entities, and it also serves to unify and regulate a society whose members are subject to a common law.

Opposite: The modest size of the wooden percussion stick is in complete contrast with the vast mass of this huge bell in Mingun, Burma, which weighs over 97 tonnes and is 3.70 m (12 ft) in height – the largest bell ever successfully cast. Despite this, repeated blows of a small mallet are enough to activate the bell, whose imposing sound was first heard in 1808.

Above: Carillon of *zhong* bells in a Confucian temple in China. Each of the bells has the ability to emit several different pitches of sound, depending on the point on which it is struck. The monk in the foreground holds a *sheng* or Chinese mouth organ.

The nomadic instrument

Unlike the instruments developed in a sedentary society, which tend to be made to a pattern, symbolizing social order and unison, there are also free-standing, lightweight instruments that are portable and not subject to any standardization either of form or the sound they produce. Each sounds precisely as its maker wants it to sound, in harmony with his voice and accompanying him everywhere. Such instruments are travelling companions; the bard keeps up a dialogue with his instrument, using it to accompany his songs and his words. In this way it echoes his voice as he proceeds on his journey, helping him to keep alive the tradition he represents.

The timbre of the instrument is the same as that of its master, whose voice is of course nothing other than the voice of his language, his land and his locality. It is the instrument that takes its cue from the man, serving him and modelling itself on him. The instrument is the 'other' voice, that echoes his own, following its modulations, embroidering and extending its line.

Nomadic lutes and fiddles are found in every corner of the world. Their morphology predisposes them to this widespread use. Hewn out of a block of green wood, without the careful preparation that would only be possible if a workshop or fixed abode were available, the body is sometimes so simple as to be almost crude, the pegs are plainly carved and the bridge is of a piece with the rest, or sometimes made of whatever suitable natural material happens to be readily available locally. Also taken from the immediate environment are the strings, often made of animal gut or vegetable fibres, and more rarely of silk.

How many such basic forms have travelled all over the Asian continent, following the Silk Road or the Spice Road. Their names are often similar even when the forms have diverged quite widely – from *setar* to *târ*, *tambur* to *tampura*, *panduri* to *dombra*, *rabab* to *rebab*, from *pipa* to guitar – as well as all those instruments resembling viols, fiddles and violins – among them *kythiak* or *kemanche*, *sarinda* or *sarangi*, *morinkhuur* or *kokyu*. When plucked or rubbed, their strings tell the history of peoples and individuals in songs, ballads, romances and epics.

They roam at will, oblivious to frontiers, sparking complicities, relationships and marriages of their own. Witness to every exchange, transaction or alliance, they sing of freedom and the wanderings of man, his adventures and his encounters with other peoples. If they break off their constant peregrinations, their voice seizes up and they lose their memory. They need to remain nomadic so that they can continue to be enriched by other repertoires, tales and songs.

Right: *Târ* lute, with six metal strings, from Qazvin in Iran. Found everywhere from Iran to the Caucasus, the *tar* was formerly associated with the 19th-century classical repertoire but is now also played at popular festivals.

Opposite: Man playing the *dümbelek* drum followed by another accompanying himself on the lute, as they proceed along a village street in the Caucasus.

Double page overleaf: A group of violin- and bass-players en route to a wedding feast near Oltenita in south-eastern Romania.

Instruments and their destinies

In the same way as it is possible to describe the evolution of a family of instruments from a crude prototype or a founding principle, so too can the geographical progress of an early instrumental type be traced through the various alliances and adoptions it contracts on its way, to the new forms that develop as a result and the new types of music they produce.

The simple musical bow – the original chordophone – is one of the oldest known instruments. Used all over the world as much for hunting as for making music, the simplest form has a string stretched between and joining together the two extremities of a flexible stick, and this is tapped or nipped, while the player's mouth serves as a resonator. It is possible to add a soundbox or resonator made of a gourd or some other material, or a number of bows may be joined together and lashed to a resonance chamber to become a pluriarc.

The musical bow occurs not only in prehistoric Europe (as evidenced by the Magdalenian depiction at Les Trois Frères, Ariège, of a horned man playing what appears to be a musical bow (see p. 21), but also in America, Africa, Oceania and Eastern Asia. It was principally on the African continent that the pluriarc, and subsequently the harp, evolved. Harps have a characteristic triangular form, with strings of varying lengths, and may be either 'arched' or 'angular'. They made their first appearance in the Sumerian world (3000 BC) and in Egypt (2700 BC), before spreading to Greece and Iran and thence throughout Asia, including India, Burma and China. In each country, the destiny of the instrument was markedly different.

It is a curious fact that certain quite elaborate early prototypes, for which we have contemporary evidence in pictorial representations dating from antiquity, have completely disappeared, while other more primitive types are still in use, usually within aboriginal populations. The obsolescence of this or that instrument is accounted for either by the disappearance of the social class that played it, and which it came to symbolize, or by the fact of being closely linked to rituals that themselves fell into disuse, or simply perhaps because of a lack of interest on the part of the musicians themselves, who may have wanted to move on and discover new sounds. Thus the number of possible scenarios for the life, evolution and disappearance of musical instruments is almost infinite.

Discovering exactly what was the fate of a particular type of instrument is often a matter of retracing the social and religious context in which it evolved. Instruments that developed within certain civilizations or social groups are directly conditioned by their environment, as is the use to which they are put. Thus an instrument that is an attribute of power can only evolve in relation to the exercise of that power, and can only last as long as it endures. Important though it may be, its disappearance becomes inevitable from the day on which the established order crumbles. Such relics include extraordinary sets of bronze bells found in archaeological excavations in China, notably in the tomb of the Marquis Yi (ruler of the petty northern state of

Preceding double page: The structure of African harps and the playing position adopted by the musicians are exactly comparable to those recorded in ancient Egyptian paintings, providing evidence of close links between the African and ancient Egyptian civilizations. Left: a blind musician depicted in the tomb of Nakht, Thebes. Right: a harpist of the Zande people (photographed in 1912). Democratic Republic of Congo.

Left: Among the Dan of the Ivory Coast, the musical bow, or *garg*, is played by hunters to ensure good hunting in the days to follow. The player places the string between his lips and strikes it with a thin stick. Modifying the volume by altering the position of his lips, and of the tongue within the mouth cavity, the musician creates different harmonics to produce a tune.

Zeng) at Leigudun (Hubei province); remarkable for their number, weight and size, these bells demonstrate the high social rank of their owner and the political and economic power he enjoyed.

More than instruments to be played, the bells represent symbols of power, suggestive of a type of music entirely identified with the particular social order and with the spatial and temporal organization subscribed to by the deceased. Because they were synonymous with a single social class and a specific ritual, such sets of bells vanished almost overnight, at a turning-point in history. One question remains, was the belief that an ensemble such as this would continue to play in the life beyond the tomb, or were the bells buried as evidence of the high civilization that produced them?

Other instruments have survived despite all manner of political and social upheavals. Instruments in popular use, like drums and flutes in particular, are still found today practically unchanged in form. Lutes and fiddles, on the other hand, which have travelled the Asian continent many times over as prized possessions of nomadic peoples subject to no law and no master, have brought change and innovation in their wake. Introduced into China by the barbarian tribes around the time of the Han dynasty, the lute called *pipa*, with its four strings, is the perfect exemplar of this new freedom of expression, being capable of producing sounds ranging from imitations of battle (with a special technique that involved striking both the belly of the instrument and the strings) to melodic playing with or without vocal accompaniment.

Lutes and fiddles

Sung poetry accompanied by a lute or a fiddle is an almost universal phenomenon common to every period, this being the musical genre that lends itself particularly to improvisation, both textual and musical, as

well as the mode of expression adopted by the bard and the troubadour. Through these performers, their roles sometimes united in one person, the development and maintenance of a whole tradition was assured, in terms of its language, its expression in song, and the music that supplied the rhythm and melodic or modal accompaniment.

There are innumerable types of lute and their derivatives, from India to Iran, the Middle East to Europe: they include the *sitar, sarod, tampura, setar, ud, târ, tanbur,* bouzouki, *cobza, saz, viela* and guitar. To this list may be added the *charango*

or *machete* of Portugal and the Azores, the plucked various chordophones of Africa, from the *dumbri* to the *kora*, not to mention the harps and lyres and the *ramkie* played in southern Africa, the *bandura* and the balalaïka from central Asia, the *ruanxian* and all the variants of the three-stringed *sanxian* in China, the *shamisen* in Japan, the four-stringed lutes 'in the shape of the moon', the *yueqin* and *cha pei*.

No less various are the fiddles: this group ranges from the Armenian/Iranian *kemanche* (meaning 'arc' or 'bow') to the *rabab*, the pattern of whose distribution extends throughout the Islamic world as far as Indonesia, becoming *rebeb* in North Africa, and the Indian fiddles the *sarinda*, *sringara* and *sarangi*, as well as the Afghan *rebab*, which resembles both the *rebec* and the European violin. Together with the Mongolian *morinkhuur* with horse's head, the Chinese *erhu*, *qinhu* and *sihu* (the term *hu* signifies 'barbarian', as these fiddles all came from the West) constitute no more than one branch of the immense family of fiddles, of different sizes, stringing and usage, which have given rise to the *kokyu* in Japan and the *sawthai* in Thailand. From the

The name *rabab* is used both for a small three-stringed lute with a pear-shaped body, and for the five-stringed Indian fiddle with a rectangular body and long neck.
Opposite: detail of an Islamic miniature (Topkapi Museum, Istanbul).
Above: detail of an Indian miniature attributed to the school of Jammu.

153

Bowed strings and plucked strings

Sarangi fiddle from the Indian state of Gujarat. The muted tone of the instrument results from a combination of animal-gut strings, which are stout but very flexible, the thick walls of the soundbox, and the narrow sounding table, which is covered with skin membrane. The sound of the bowed strings is augmented by the tinkling of small bells attached to the bow. L. 62 cm (24½ in.).

Hatun charango lute from Chuquisaca in Bolivia. The powerful sound of this lute, which is used at major public festivals like Carnival, is produced by its set of five double strings made of metal. The brightly coloured decoration of the wooden neck is appropriate for occasions of celebration and rejoicing. L. 98 cm (38½ in.).

Viola de cocho lute from Mato Grosso state, Brazil. The neck and large soundbox are carved from a single block of wood. Four thin nylon strings extend over a wide sounding board which contains no soundhole, resulting in a rather muffled sound. The quietness of these instruments, which are often played in ensembles, makes them particularly well suited to accompanying singers' voices. L. 75 cm (29½ in.).

Sarangi fiddle from Rajasthan, India. The four animal-gut strings are stretched by means of four round-headed pegs. All the other pegs attached to the neck and upper part of the pegbox are used to tighten and tune the thirty-five sympathetic strings. The muted sound of the main strings, which are played with a horsehair bow, combines harmoniously with the hum arising from the spontaneous vibration of the metal strings. L. 65 cm (25½ in.).

Caucasus to Bulgaria, the *fandur, lira, lirica, gadulka* and *gusla* also bear a strong resemblance to one another, notwithstanding their individual features. The *gadulka*, for example, has sympathetic strings and is held vertically, resting on the player's knee; the *gusla*, however, has only one string made of twisted horsehair. And finally, there are the many sorts of primitive fiddle which contributed to the development of the European violin, among them the Norwegian Hardanger fiddle with sympathetic strings, the variety of instruments from the Middle Ages called *fidel* or *fithele*, as well as the *lira di braccio* and the *lira di gamba*, mother of the violoncello. This vast family of instruments exemplifies a function of music that has nothing to do with ritual, social hierarchies or codifications of any kind. Sounds can have so powerful an impact on the senses and the human spirit that their role was regarded originally, within a society where order prevailed and every individual fulfilled his allotted role, as being to communicate directly with the divinity. In the course of time, as events dictated – and very much at the whim of nature and the vagaries of man's creative spirit – instruments began to be made by people for their own use, a development paralleled by the rise of religions that allowed a direct relationship between the individual and his god or gods. Such emancipation and the potential for all to seek personal salvation engendered a desire for freedom, and this in turn unleashed other forces which had until then remained latent, contained within the sacred ritual and exercised only through the offices of a benevolent monarch.

As he became conscious of his individual destiny, man regained possession of those things that society had previously administered for him as a member of a community. Free from constant supervision, left to his own devices and exposed to the uncertainties of life no longer cushioned by a womb-like predictability, man discovered and exploited his own musical potential. It was in the context of such creativity that musical instruments became something more than an attribute or an apparatus used in the service of a form of music dictated to man by the heavens. In his wanderings around the world and explorations of its mysteries, man acquired a divinity of his own and, in communion with an instrument, discovered and developed a language other than words through which to express the inexpressible. The recourse to inspiration led him to experiment with a new dimension, and he began to make music.

The soul of the violin

No instrument has better served instinctive musical creativity than the violin. Whether used to accompany the voice or dance, or given complete freedom, it allows the player to echo the voice and extend its range to the point at which scarcely a nuance of the soul or sentiments is left unexpressed. Even in an interpretation of music written by a composer, with a score to refer to, no one performer's touch will be exactly the same as another, and often an instrumentalist is as easily identified by his playing as by his outward appearance.

Above: *Violoncellista Crepax* by Anselmo Bucci (1887–1955). The Western instrumentalist is in a situation quite unlike that of musicians in civilizations having an oral tradition. He or she must interpet music, almost every aspect of which is already specified in the printed score.

Opposite: In spite of its simple appearance, the *erhu* fiddle produces a rich and expressive sound, making it an essential member of both classical and popular ensembles in China; it is also employed as a solo instrument which allows long melodic improvisations.

Double page overleaf: Musicians in a town square in the Czech Republic. The versatility of stringed instruments is shown to best advantage in their repertoire of popular tunes. The style of playing features rapid bowstrokes, alternating with long, plaintive passages of rubato.

The nomadic violin

The Fiddler by Marc Chagall, oil on canvas, 184 x 148.5 cm (72½ x 58½ in.),

1912-13.

Stedelijk Museum, Amsterdam

The violin is the instrument of nomadic peoples, and it also expresses the soul of the Wandering Jew seeking his place in the world, the promised land. His fiddle represents that empty space, it sings of the perfect place where, ultimately, the chosen and martyred people – outcasts touched with genius, and in particular a genius for music – will be able to settle.

Above the icy rooftops, in a land where the skies are black and the ground is covered in snow, above the closed-up cottages, a figure dances between heaven and earth while watching over his sleeping companions as he communes with the Eternal, who dictates to him his laws through the song of the violin. By the power of his music, he is raised to the top of the holy mountain, and he captures the divine message in the playing of his instrument.

The essence of music is expressed through improvisation – everything the musician has acquired in respect of technique, as well as everything he has drawn from tradition, and developed and enriched in the course of fulfilling his destiny on earth. All of this underpins his inspiration, which is spontaneous and expresses itself without the aid of any written or memorized text, and which is ephemeral and leaves no visible trace. Yet the manner of expressing his inspiration is deeply ingrained in the musician's mind.

Notes of music transmit the inexpressible; they can revive impressions obliterated by time, forgotten by the senses but imprinted on the heart more securely than they could ever be on any score, because they were created by that inspiration which raises the musician, through his instrument, towards a sublimation of his being.

All the repertoires are available to the violin – from Indian music, which is essentially colour and mode, with no score and no playing from memory, to gypsy airs in which rhythm and tempo are once again not regulated by written music but instead rely on a well perfected tradition of playing by ear. Numerous European composers have tried to capture this nomadic music by transcribing it and adapting it for full orchestra, producing a greatly increased volume to recreate something of its original power. Composers like Liszt, Brahms, Bartók, Smetana, Dvořák, Chopin, Grieg, Sibelius and Kodály all had a special interest in folk dances and popular songs.

As a solo instrument following a melodic line, the violin can convey every imaginable shade of feeling. Or it can accompany the piano in a sonata for two voices, combine with viola and cello in a quartet in complete symbiosis with the other instruments, or respond to the orchestra, expressing every aspect of the human condition, be it heart-wrenching, yearning, triumphant and solitary. Its potential for improvisation and dynamic phrasing have led it to be used occasionally in jazz, where it can be particularly effective as a partner in blues and vocals, paraphrasing and weaving its free variations.

The roving guitar

Other types of instrument whose use has become universal possess a similarly complex genealogy. That is certainly true of the guitar, whose form as well as its name betrays the influence of its various ancestors. Although it is a member of the family of plucked chordophones from Central Asia, it is also in a direct line of descent from the zither – as its name indicates, one of its forebears being the Greek *kithara*.

The form of the *târ* of Armenia and Iran – regions that formerly constituted a natural crossroads for human migrations – was disseminated both to the West and to eastern Asia. Its 'waisted' body in the shape of two hearts subsequently became a feature of viols and guitars in the West. Its name, too, was spread abroad, and in various forms would come to designate many different kinds of Asian lute, both long- and short-necked, which travelled the Silk Road. From the *dotar* ('two strings') and *setar* ('three strings') it became the Indian *sitar*, then in China during the Han dynasty, it turned into *pipa* – a name that would appear to be onomatopœic, referring to the sound that it makes, or derived at least from an onomatopœic name of origin – before becoming *biwa* in Japan, where it first made its appearance towards the end of the Tang dynasty, in the tenth century.

Moving further to the west, the distant ancestors of the guitar were the Arab lute, the gittern, the *mandore*, the cither, and more recently the Renaissance *vihuela* and the Italian *chitarra battente*. After many migrations and with contributions from elsewhere, the European guitar began to be differentiated and to emerge in a recognizable form, with musical genres of its own, towards the end of the fifteenth century. It was adopted by poets to accompany their verses and ballads, madrigals and *canciones*, Moorish

Left: Group of Mexican musicians in Chiapas state. The player of the *guitarrón*, who is laying down the bass line, is flanked by two other musicians playing the melody on fiddles whose design is based on that of the classic Western violin.

as well as Spanish, and no sooner were its metamorphoses complete than it continued its migrations across the oceans. Transported to the New World at the time of the Spanish conquest, it was adopted in all regions of the Americas, in new forms and fulfilling new functions, proof yet again of an adaptability unique in the history of musical instruments: variants included the jumbo, *dobro*, ukelele or banjo, banjolele and *mandolinetto*. In Brazil, it was *violão* or *viola de cocho*, in Chile the *guitarrón*, in Argentina the *charango*.

The peregrinations of the guitar perfectly exemplify the destiny of the nomadic instrument, infinitely adaptable and an indispensable companion to its owner. Of all instruments it seems the one best suited as a vehicle for free expression, as practised by a person who, capable of being in direct communication with tradition, appoints himself to sing the praises of a particular way of life. Released from the restrictive social ties that would keep him within the orbit of some authority requiring allegiance and submission, and having become a social outcast by his own choosing, that individual acquires – albeit at the price of very real insecurity and discomfort – an autonomy that makes him conscious of his unfettered freedom as a traveller. Beyond languages, beyond techniques, beyond styles, the guitar communicates in a manner which everyone can understand; it has no fixed rules and therefore knows no frontiers. It is within reach of all thanks to its size, because it is easily obtainable and because it is easy to play. The sound of its soft, vibrant timbre affects the listener as much as it does the player. The physical proximity of the soundbox that transmits the impact of the notes to the musician makes the guitar an eminently sensual instrument, both in terms of handling and sound, especially when compared to the violin, which is more cerebral and has, at least in the Western world, to be held in a less comfortable position, with the resonating table touching only the chin.

Flutes: enchantment or devilry

Whether an instrument is considered to have masculine or feminine qualities, and the social role allotted to it – these are factors that will have a considerable influence on its future, more even than its evolution in strictly musical terms.

The flute was the first true instrument. Effectively a transitional object between man and nature, it was universally used to mimic birdsong, and thereby influenced human singing. Utilized for musical purposes from the Palaeolithic era onwards, it had pastoral associations in antiquity and was regarded as an enchantress capable of casting spells and seducing the listener, whether animal or human. In so-called 'primitive' civilizations, it is considered a sacred instrument to be kept hidden away; essentially an extension of the

mask, the flute is viewed as a magical attribute. Although numerous legends describe the flute as having a seductive (and by implication feminine) voice, and although most peoples associate it with rituals, divinities and meditation, within certain traditional societies it is played almost exclusively by men, presumably because of its phallic form – in the same way as the rounded shape of the drum is associated with a woman's belly. The musical duo of flute and drum in fact make up the perfect couple, much in evidence in popular festivals worldwide. And yet this ancient instrument, revered in certain cultures for its ability to ward off evil and evil spells, is entirely absent from Christian liturgical music. Presumably the exclusion of

Opposite: Kayan flautist in Sarawak, Malaysia. Flutes of this sort are improvised intruments, made for the occasion. They consist simply of a hollow plant stem with a round opening cut to form a blowing hole.

Below: Fisherman playing the *pincullo* recorder in Bolivia. This type of flute is both durable and portable, making it the ideal instrument for nomads and those obliged by the nature of their work to be constantly on the move.

Double page overleaf: For as long as anyone can remember tunes played on the pipe have been used to accompany the regular beat of marching feet: (left) a musician playing the double flute or oboe, depicted in an Etruscan painting in the Tomb of the Leopards at Tarquinia, (c. 490 BC); (right) a Quechua boy playing the *quena* as he strides along the road to Cuzco, Peru.

the flute from churches and temples has not a little to do with the profane character of popular music and the pagan nature of ancient or non-Christian rites which clings to it by association.

Light in weight, easily transported and not subject to complicated sets of rules, because anyone who wants to make music can fashion his own instrument, the flute is essentially nomadic. Yet its history has been quite different in the Far East, where it has been regarded since time immemorial as the embodiment of fundamental musical pitch, and played therefore in association with other instruments. Ancient Chinese legends describe how it was made from a length of bamboo as a means of measuring sounds based on the song of the male and female phoenix.

Symptomatic of the desire for solid, weighty objects symbolizing law and power are bells, which in both the East and the West have tended to replace pipes because they produce a more imposing and resonant sound, whether conveying messages or summonses, signalling the hours, or even defining the intervals of the musical scale.

Very few instruments have been allowed a regular place in Christian temples and churches alongside the bells that serve as guardians of temporal and spiritual power. If the slender, lightweight flute is represented at all, it is through the organ-pipe, the organ having served for nearly a millennium as the principal instrumental accompaniment to the liturgy. The ultimate descendant of the flute, however, was not the medieval portative organ but the harmonium, an instrument of the accordion family developed in the early nineteenth century. The instrument's three main constituents are its ranks of free reeds, keys and bellows, combining the principle of the ancient *aulos* or double-reed pipe, the reservoir of air as found in the mouth-organs of eastern Asia, and the keyboard and playing position of the piano. Its full sound required a suitable interior space and a particular acoustic, and it found its perfect accommodation in churches and places of worship.

Piano and *forte*

The harpsichord having been regarded as a symbol of the nobility under the Ancien Régime, many instruments were destroyed at the time of the French Revolution. Others were painted black to disguise their true identity or perhaps consigned to the attic, there to lie forgotten. Now, the piano took its place as the new keyboard instrument of the bourgeoisie. Women and girls would be encouraged to sit at the keyboard in a decorous posture and show off their skills, given that no unseemly physical contortions were involved and the shape of the piano had no obvious sexual connotations.

Mademoiselle Gachet at the Piano, detail of the painting by Vincent van Gogh, 1890. After the French Revolution, the piano began to supersede the harpsichord and other keyboard instruments and make its appearance in the living rooms of the bourgeoisie. It was regarded as particularly suitable for women because the playing posture conformed with the social etiquette of the day.

The harpsichord had helped revive a repertoire of old songs, rustic interludes, peasant dances and sarabandes, which became popular diversions at court. The piano, with its more universal appeal, found itself in vogue when Romanticism was at its height, and was therefore destined more than any other instrument for the expression and sublimation of individual feelings. Being polyphonic, it was self-sufficient and needed no accompaniment.

The piano, then, indicated a return to more substantial keyboard instruments intended for domestic use – it was as though anyone who was able to afford a piano (regardless of ability to play it) could join the bourgeois establishment. Ownership of such an instrument was a sign of social success, or of the operation of democracy.

The development in the West of the tonal scale regularized music by restricting composition to a certain number of permitted notes. This desire to control the potential of sound was compounded by enclosing it within a box, and by confining musical genres as well within strict forms that could not be varied by the musical enthusiast. All this was done in the name of established and accepted theory. By contrast, any other sort of music could only appear disorganized, undisciplined and primitive. The ear, trained to hear only fixed intervals, lost its acuity and took refuge in a precisely regulated repertoire, so that those conditioned to listen in this way believed no other possible form of music but their own could exist. The result was a sort of musical ethnocentrism: people who encountered different sorts of music came to think of and treat its exponents almost as they might enemies on a battlefield.

This isolation dogged Western musicians for centuries, a handicap that was experienced with particular force at the time of Bonaparte's expedition to Egypt in 1798. Among the band of French scholars who accompanied the army was Guillaume-André Villoteau. He had joined the choir school of Notre-Dame and had sung in the chorus of the Opéra-Comique. Now, like the other members of the expedition, he found himself listening for the first time to the alien sound of Egyptian music. Only gradually, and above all because of his desire to commit what he heard to paper, did he overcome his aversion to this labyrinth of sounds and discover in it a 'guiding thread' that indicated to him that he was not hearing random combinations of notes, but evidence of a firm and precise musical structure.

Such an insight into other musical worlds was a step in the direction of reaching a new understanding, and probably constituted one of the most positive developments arising from this expedition to Egypt. Thanks to the new perspective that resulted, the influence of so-called 'exotic' music came to be felt increasingly in Western music, for example in piano works by Debussy.

The Violin (detail) by Juan Gris, 1916. In the first half of the 20th century, the radical movements in art that transformed painting were paralleled by major experimental developments in Western music.

Antique score

Paean to Apollo by Tynnichus and finale of *Ajax Furioso* by Timotheus of Miletus

(c. 450–360 BC), papyrus, c. AD 160.

Staatliche Museen, Berlin

For centuries music was transmitted orally from one generation to the next. The musician was the sole repository of musical knowledge that would only later be written down by different individuals concerned with notation, composition, the technique of instrumental playing and musical embellishment, song and voice inflection, etc. Thus, in pre-Imperial China, the responsibility for memorizing all these things and maintaining all these skills rested fairly and squarely on the shoulders of the practising musician, who was preferably a blind man with a heightened sense of hearing.

In ancient Greece most of the so-called lyric poets composed their words while accompanying themselves on the lyre or the *barbitos* (with longer strings), although the musical element of these poems has often been lost. The poets needed to be composers, instructors and instrumentalists all at once, but the laws of harmony necessary for written transposition were the business of the *mousikos*, with a specialist knowledge of intervals, scales, rhythms and the combining of instruments. It seems that a rudimentary system of musical notation had been developed in the sixth century BC by Pythagoras himself, while a century later the compositions of Pindar were circulating throughout the Greek world; by the time of the score for Euripides' *Orestes*, the system had been perfected. The treatise by Alypius gives some clues to the decoding of this system of transcription – the notes being accompanied by signs indicating exact pitch within a scale or mode – but this procedure was aimed more at keeping a written record of a work than at making a decipherable musical score.

Certain works by Timotheus of Miletus, a lyrical composer of dithyrambs and nomes, were reset and adapted by later musicians. The score represented here is an autograph composition by one of these later musicians – an indication perhaps of the freedom with which works that came to be considered classics were adapted to suit the taste of the day.

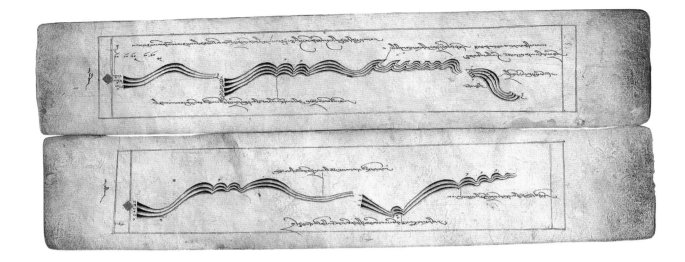

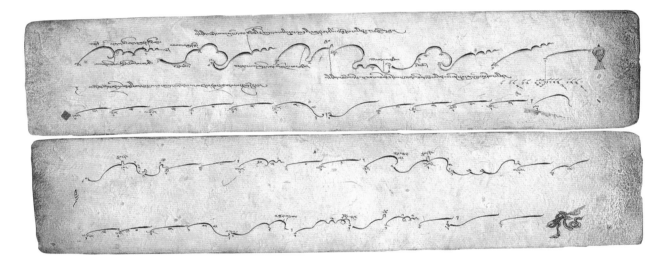

Musical notation

It was indeed the encounter with music deemed to be 'different' that provided the initial impetus and justification for attempts at musical notation. Retranscribing such music in terms of one's own cultural codes, although it may involve the need for a degree of adaptation, does at least have the effect of making the result intellectually respectable, even if the listener's ear still has difficulty in coming to terms with it.

It is in performing such an exercise that the ethnomusicologist learns to 'recognize' music and thus ascribe an identity to it. Of course this music did not have to await the arrival of the professional ethnomusicologist before coming into existence, and it can manage perfectly well without his 'recognition'; the fact remains, however, is that the ethnological process – in the sphere of music in particular – by memorizing traditional structures, tends to extend their lives, at least as models, and it holds up a mirror for their own contemplation.

It has always fallen to an outside eye to evaluate, assess and record information, establishing the criteria and working out a system by which to interpret data. Whether it concerns folk music collected in the field, or music written down according to an accepted convention, the procedure adopted is identical, or at least based on the same system.

Ideally, of course, each type of music should be noted down according to a method that reflects its distinctive features. Certain peoples have thus developed their own musical language which is an extension of their spoken and written language. Each culture has a different voice, a different way of speaking and a different approach to music; hence its system of writing, if it has one, will be peculiar to it, and not capable of being applied to another culture in a fully consistent manner. It seems hardly appropriate, for example, to use a Western system of notation to transcribe music in which improvisation is the basis of expression and the rhythm so complex as to go beyond anything the standard signs used in European music can begin to convey. The use of Western methods in other musical traditions would be more than merely restrictive, it would be altogether misleading.

Villoteau's pioneering experience when confronted with Egyptian music still has many lessons for us: the 'guiding thread' that justified the scholar's intervention was identified by the process of memorizing what he heard. It was only when he realized that he could recognize a tune, because he had heard the same sound before, that he could listen properly and with due attention. To be readily accessible, a tune first needs to be properly assimilated in the mind of the listener. 'Recognition' signifies that, having once committed a tune to memory, one has the ability to reproduce it. There is nothing to say that such attempts at reproduction will be a perfect reflection of the original, but at least they will offer as faithful an imitation as possible.

The process of learning to read and interpret the systems of notation peculiar to a culture is as complicated as that of learning the alphabet. Sometimes there are musical criteria that have no equivalent in any other culture. For the most part, there are only partial clues that are difficult to decipher by anyone other than those who actually play the music. The notation offers a guiding thread for the words and rhythm and for some of the notes, but rarely for the whole. In addition, if the system of musical notation has been designed for a particular instrument, there will also be indications about playing technique which demand specialized interpretation.

Oral and written traditions

In most of the great traditions, music has remained alive because it has been memorized and transmitted orally from one generation to the next. If writing had a role to play, it was principally to note down the words of songs, which

later became poems if people no longer knew how they should be sung. As for the music that accompanied these words, it was usually only written down much later, and as a consequence it was probably much simplified and considerably impoverished.

Writing down music to ensure its survival leaves little more than the bare bones of a skeleton which the musician has to bring back to life. Usually musical traditions remain alive only if they are thriving; writing them down tends to ossify them and hasten their end. The dynamic is lost in the process of committing them to paper. Hence, in the context of traditional music, notation should be no more than a form of partial aide-mémoire, an imperfect attempt, a sort of concession that falls short of a full interpretation of the music achieved by playing it. Sometimes musical rules have actually been established after the event, solely in order to keep a written record of the characteristics of a certain sort of music.

In fact there exist almost as many systems of notation as there are types of music and musical instruments, with indications of playing techniques included within the musical score. There are cases where only instrumental technique is noted, implying an apprenticeship with a master who transmits the music orally. Or occasionally, the words of a song and the technique employed for the instrumental accompaniment may be transcribed, but not the music itself.

An apprentice musician familiarizing himself with the harp, Central Africa. Mastering a musical instrument can take years of practice, during which the future instrumentalist attempts to reproduce the gestures of more experienced players .

Double page overleaf: Young boys of the Dan people in the Ivory Coast learn music by playing on miniature instruments specially made for children. From left to right and top to bottom: small drum made from the stem and leaf of a bamboo; wooden drum; bark zither; gourds held between the children's legs in the manner adopted by adults playing the *baa* drum; musical bow resting against an enamel bowl; xylophone supported on a child's legs.

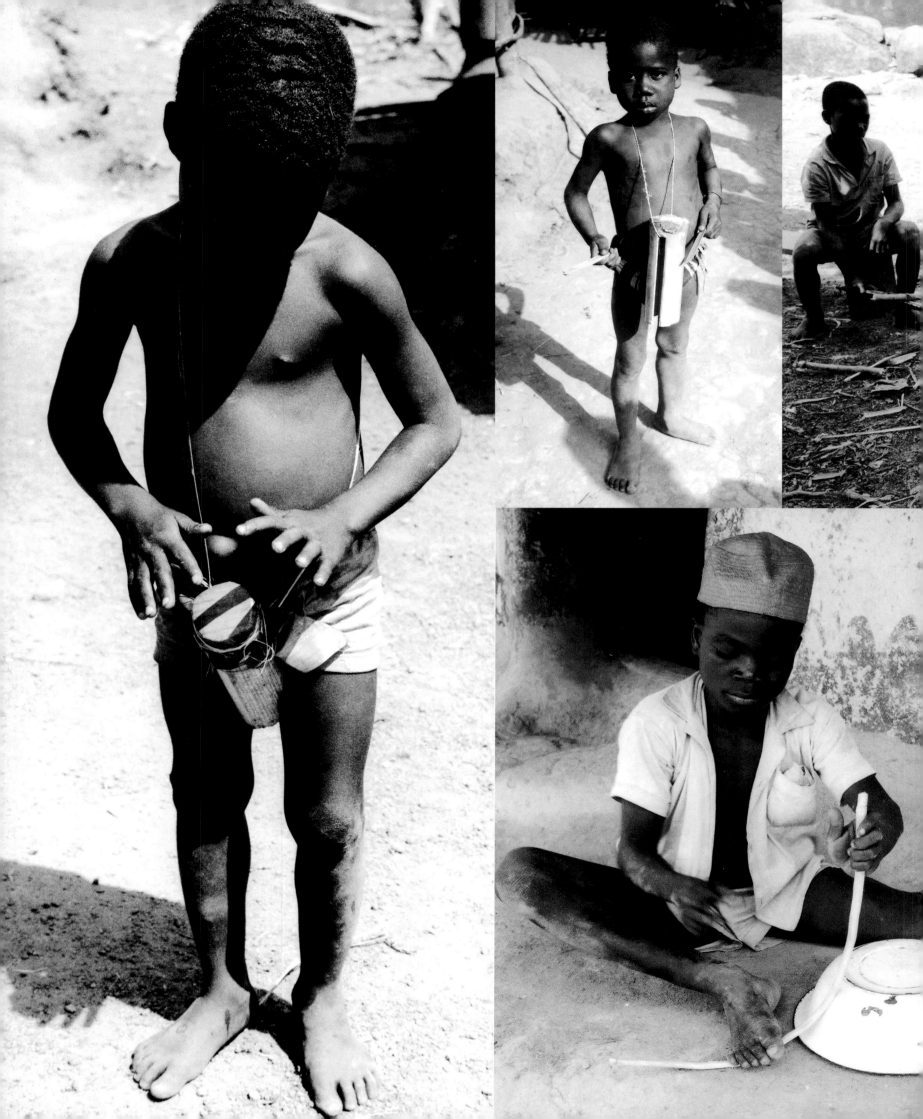

Kettledrum played in Madras, India, utilizing an old earthenware kitchen pot for the body. The stretched skin membrane is struck with tongues of soft leather. H. 12 cm (4¾ in.); D. 19 cm (7½ in.).

Spoons used in Turkey for serving olives: when placed back to back and tapped alternately against the palm of the hand and the thigh, they are transformed into hollow idiophones. L. 28 cm (11 in.).

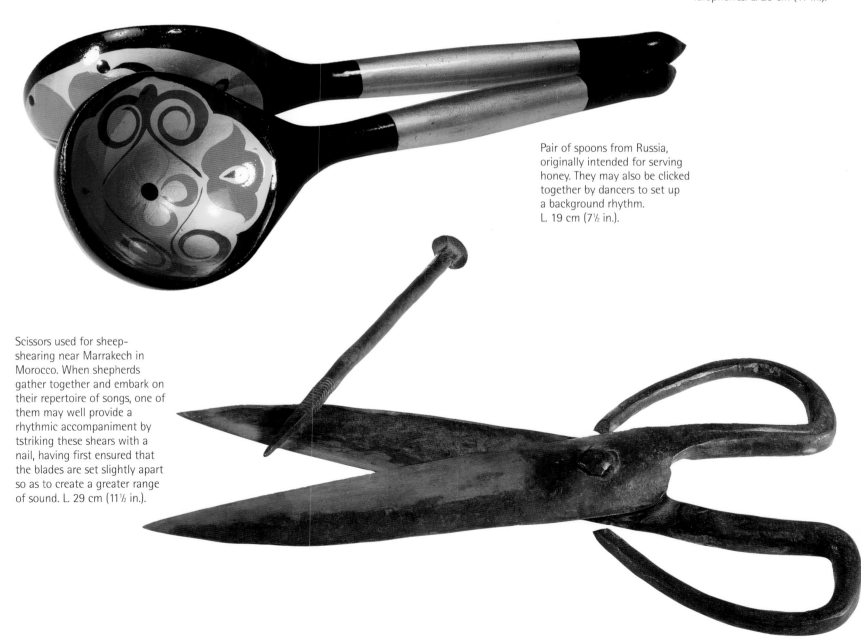

Pair of spoons from Russia, originally intended for serving honey. They may also be clicked together by dancers to set up a background rhythm. L. 19 cm (7½ in.).

Scissors used for sheep-shearing near Marrakech in Morocco. When shepherds gather together and embark on their repertoire of songs, one of them may well provide a rhythmic accompaniment by tstriking these shears with a nail, having first ensured that the blades are set slightly apart so as to create a greater range of sound. L. 29 cm (11½ in.).

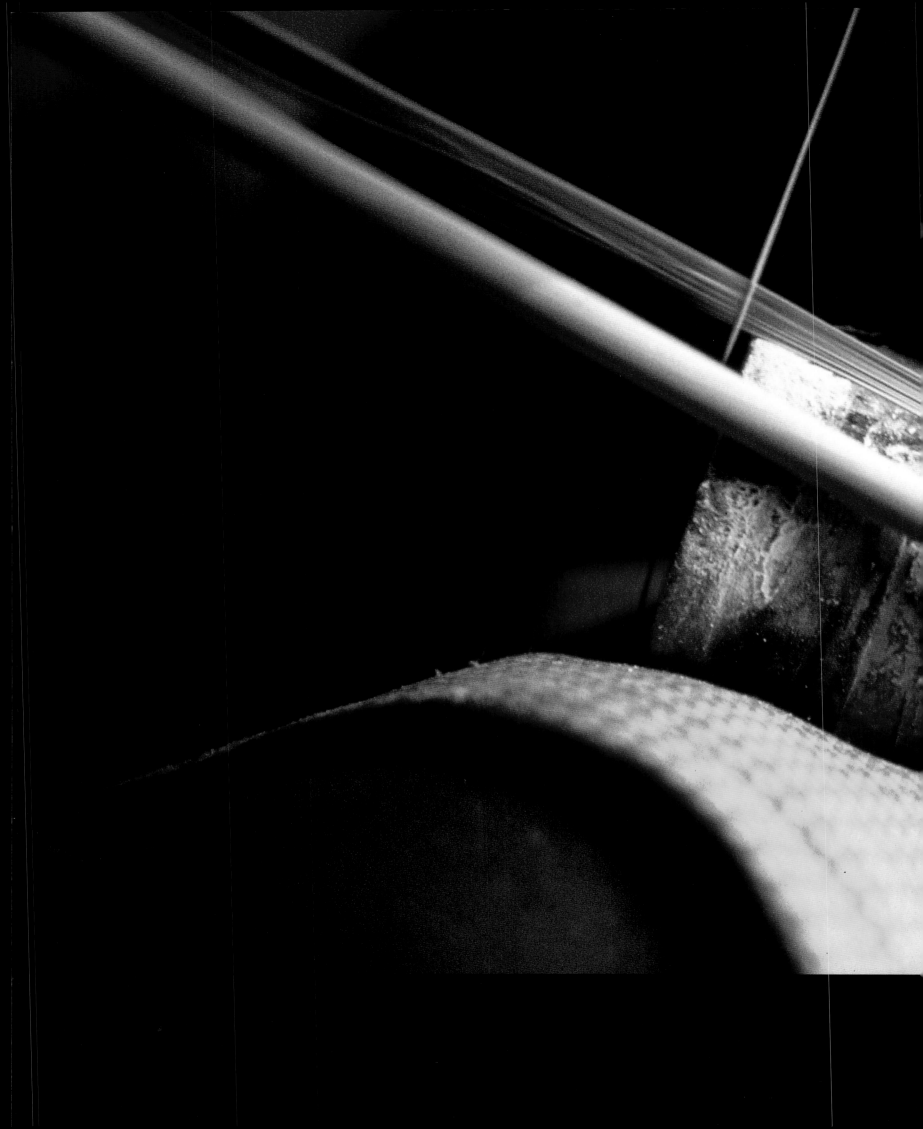

5 Giving Matter a Soul

All matter is consciousness

First, man took note of sounds and explored their origins
in the mineral, vegetable or animal kingdoms, then he
used them to tame his environment, and having begun to
understand them and how to control them, he defined his
place in the world by taking up a position between nature
and its manifestations. As a means of fulfilling his desire to
comprehend and participate in the world order, sound must
have seemed the ideal intermediary between natural forces
and human needs. This was now the time for him to be
creative, to invent new forms, to intervene in the natural
order of things and discover new domains of sound. Having
once acquired a technology with almost unlimited potential,
Homo sapiens turned to making instruments to fulfil his
ambition. Thus the dawn of consciousness was closely
followed by the advent of knowledge and science, the
means by which man would be empowered to organize
the world to his own advantage.

Master of the elements

Whereas the musical sounds had hitherto been the result
of natural phenomena – a magical form bearing a coded
message – they now made their appearance through the
agency of human artefacts. The arrival of man-made
instruments represented the supplanting and indeed
deliberate transcending of nature by human values.
Music would henceforth exist only as the result of
human involvement now that man had learned to master
the elements which had once presided over his emergence
as a conscious being. Perhaps this represented a human
victory over inanimate forces, or perhaps man merely
judged it to be so.

To begin with, sounds emitted by supra-human forces
were venerated through the natural phenomena that gave
rise to them, but they would come to be seen as proofs of

man's ability – physical realities that he could manipulate
at will. This change effectively translated the elements of
the sacred, mythical and ritual domains into attributes of
humanity, not the other way round. To compensate for
the wholesale takeover, human activities acquired a
corresponding duty to respect nature, by drawing their
inspiration from it and paying it homage in return. To
ignore nature would be to deny the origins of sound.

The instrument is transitional in the sense that it
embodies the gradual change from one era to another: it
supplies evidence of the existence of an original form, the
memory of a symbolism now lost to the human ear; it is
matter that has been transformed, yet continues to bear the
imprint of its former state; and an object marked by cultural
shifts, now orientated towards the understanding of man as
he aspires to a music of his own making.

Man uses musical instruments precisely to achieve that
end. Could we devise a better word to describe such
material artefacts, in all their forms and variants? To speak
of a 'musical instrument' is not particularly revealing, and as
a convenient label it is neither concise nor accurate. Why is
it that we have never come up with a better term, without
the use of circumlocutions? Most of the world's languages
convey the meaning in the same way, the more or less
universal formula being 'instrument [or "tool" or "utensil"]
conceived for the making of music'. There are rare
exceptions: in Armenian for example, mother language as it
is, a single word with a precise semantic significance is used
to mean musical instrument – *navarakan*. However, the
majority of languages retain the concept of an arsenal of
instruments made by man as the means of producing
sounds: music is envisaged as the end, and the instrument
as the means to that end. In general, it can be said that the
history of any man-made object sheds light above all on
the culture of the people who created it.

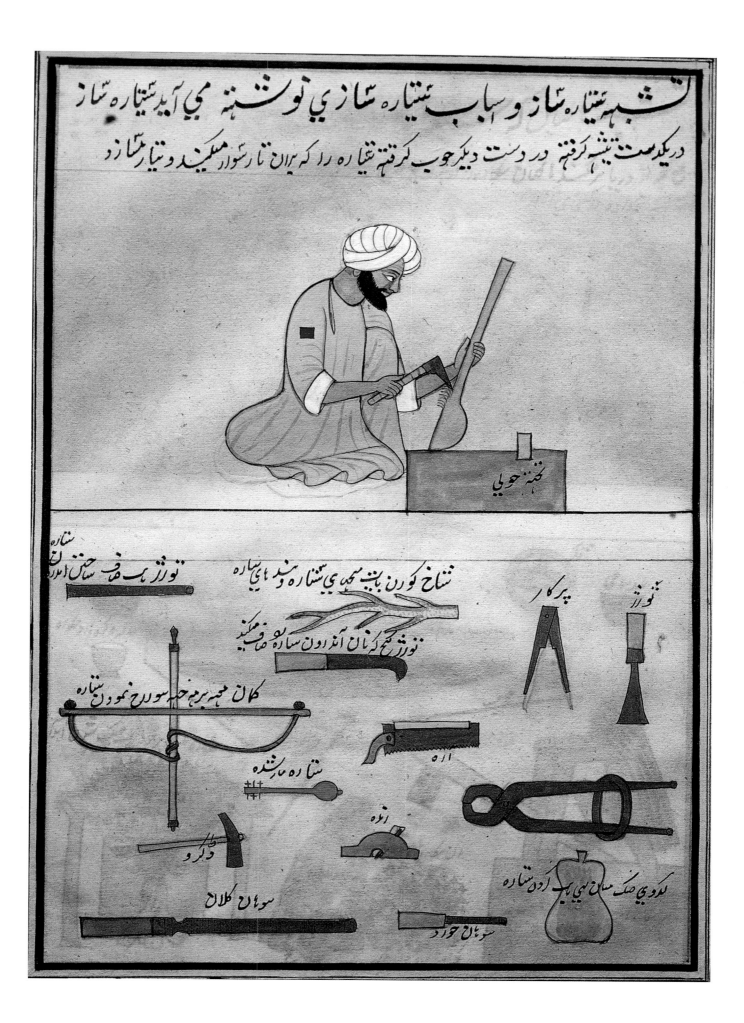

The inspiration of the muse

It is certainly possible to regard music as being a physical phenomenon just like any other. It is also possible to narrow or expand that definition, according to circumstances, and see music as a mode of expression available to all thinking men, one which relies on the use of instruments for its implementation. Its principal purpose, then, would be the provision of supreme and subtle pleasure, it would represent a culminating achievement of human civilization as well as a major contribution to it; music is as much a mark of an advanced society as some exquisite piece of jewelry. Do we not speak of 'playing an instrument'? The use of this expression without reference to technique suggests a random activity, something quite superficial, with no overriding aim other than to provide a pleasant diversion.

But human inspiration, in so far as music is concerned, has ceased to be simply a matter of organizing sounds to achieve a pantheistic harmony, it has become instead a novel form of dialogue with a superior consciousness, one that reveals to man a whole new dimension, an expansion of his capabilities and a manner of transcending the basic human condition.

This is the process of musical composition, in which sounds of every sort are integrated, or brought into play,

within the whole. This means not only those reproduced from nature but also, and chiefly, those invented to create impressions that go beyond the palette of natural sounds, or that sublimate it by their emotional content. In a sense one might say that through his skills the instrument maker accomplishes the same effect as natural resonance, but in reverse. The hand of man intervenes to make use of matter, to fashion it in such a way as to create something, and to produce sound.

The instrument maker dedicates himself to this human endeavour of creating sounds, transcribing human emotions and expressing what is inexpressible in words by the use of the appropriate tool. What he brings to the task is not just a passion to communicate all of nature's works, the physical science of instrumental acoustics and musical inspiration that is supra-human, but also his own personal state of mind and feelings.

The music that comes into his mind, inspired by the muse, appeals to him in his capacity as the good and faithful workman, and to the object that is the medium for these emotions and messages. It is not, as was the case in primeval times, the mysterious echo that speaks with the 'other' voice, but the object — and expressed in a language that is aimed directly at the senses and the mind of the listener, for no sooner are its sound vibrations emitted than

Interiors of musical instrument makers' workshops in Central Asia (opposite: Kashgar in Sinkiang province, China) and North Africa (above: Marrakech, Morocco). Everywhere the instrument maker has the same objectives: to fashion his materials in such a way as to create an instrument that expresses, both visually and musically, the aesthetic values of his culture.

The living power of the instrument

Among the rituals associated with the making of musical instruments is the introduction of something derived from a living being that is believed to animate the material object. Animal or human blood is often sprinkled on wood or the membrane used in the making of drums, in the manner of a baptism. Among the Banyankole of Uganda, when the skin of a drum is changed in preparation for a ceremonial occasion, the blood of a young boy is combined with that of a cow and with papyrus ash, and the resulting mixture is rubbed on the instrument.

In New Guinea, the membrane of the drum is glued down with lime and blood derived from the male sexual organ. Sometimes a piece of panther skin impregnated with blood is placed inside the drum and 'fed' with pimento, or the drum may be decorated with spots of blood, in imitation of a panther's skin, or a human bone may be placed inside.

Among the Bantu people, there is a taboo stating that when the skin of the drum is ruptured, no one may look inside. Although the nature of the contents is supposed to be kept secret, it is said that when the drum was made, either a large ball or else the head of a defeated enemy was placed inside. Only a particular instrument maker invited to repair the instrument is allowed to work on it.

When human sacrifices were made in ancient Mexico, the victims were laid on top of wooden drums, *teponazli*, into which their blood would drain. Most wooden drums contained the heads or jawbones of enemies defeated in combat. Anyone who had not first made an offering of a head to such a drum was forbidden to see the instrument. The sculpted motifs that occur on many of these drums depict rows of jawbones and crania, motifs reminiscent of these practices.

There are innumerable oral accounts of sacrificial practices linked to the manufacture or the baptism of musical instruments. These customs were not only sacred but so secret that they were perpetuated in the absence of any written record to confirm their existence. When bells were cast, it was the practice in some Western countries to sacrifice a black chicken or a black sheep, by throwing the animal into the molten metal. These rituals served the purpose of exorcizing evil, and represented the symbolic victory of the eminently Christian symbol of the bell over the inanimate materials, which were infused with the blood and the life-force of the animals selected as sacrificial victims. Similar rituals are practised in parts of Africa, where it falls to the blacksmith to sacrifice the animals – often cockerels, which are decapitated – so that their blood will nourish the metal and give it life.

These traditional customs recur in many other parts of the world. At Kyongju in Korea is the sacred bell of king Songdok, which dates from the eighth century; this is probably one of the most imposing examples in terms of sheer size, being 3.33 metres (nearly 11 ft) in height and weighing about 23 tonnes. Legend has it that as the molten bronze was being poured a young girl was sacrificed to ensure that the casting of the bell would be a success.

The Dan people of the Ivory Coast regard instruments as symbolic ritual objects. The drum *glong* for example, is no longer used for musical purposes but only as an altar for offering food to the gods. First a chicken is sacrificed, then cola nuts are set out, to represent raw food; next come cooked foods, such as a dish of rice with a sauce.

they are picked up by an organism that is sensitive and receptive to them.

The notion of the sacred is intensely real to the musician who surrenders himself unreservedly to his interpretation and allows himself to be carried away, just as the composer of the work had originally abandoned himself to his inspiration. It is the work itself that plays through both of them, conveyed through the voice of the chosen instrument, in what becomes both a celebration of and a sacred offering to nature.

Certainly the low booming sound produced by this bell has a particularly emotional effect on those who hear it. The bell is also thought to protect the population and ward off evil. Examples of this symbolic conjunction of metal and blood are found in most regions of the world. The two elements, one born of a fusion of materials extracted from the earth and the other a vital body fluid, are also frequently combined in initiation rituals, ceremonies associated with rites of passage and exorcisms.

Whatever the material to which the animal or human blood was added, the two substances were usually combined so as to allow them to work on one another, like living forces; the raw material is supposed to be changed by the potency of the more refined material, so that its soul is awakened and its voice unleashed.

The right material for the right sound

There are some materials that are the stuff of legend, being particularly prized for their acoustic qualities. In the Chinese tradition, many fables have grown up around the central myth of the mulberry, a tree formerly regarded as the dwelling place of the sun; its wood was supposedly used to make the zithers *qin* and *se*, while other sources refer to a pawlonia, the trunk of which was employed especially in the production of chordophones. In much same way, the Yakut shaman selects wood from a tree that has been struck by lightning to make the frame of his drum. For the person making the instrument, the vital consideration is to tap the living forces of nature. Only by doing this can he ensure that the sound the instrument produces will, in its turn, have an effect on nature.

The legends surrounding the making of musical instruments are much the same at all times and in all places. The choice of materials by instrument makers, however, depends primarily on the local ecosystem. Each place will tend to support a particular kind of instrument, depending on geographical factors and the available flora and fauna. In general, however, the relevant factors will be orientation (of a tree or plant, etc.), suitability of terrain (mountain, valley, cavern), the presence of light or shade, depending on ground cover (forest, wood, copse), the proximity of rivers or lakes, and the particular atmosphere created by all these elements in combination. Other factors include the murmur of water, the presence of birds or animals which inhabit a particular place and enliven it with their cries and activity, so providing evidence of a hospitable or attractive environment. The requirement, for the instrument maker, is to seek favourable sites that combine particular qualities, and where he can find all manner of suitable materials such as wood, stone, fruit husks, reeds, bamboos or gourds, from which to obtain the best resonances.

Wooden drums in 1887 on the island of Malekula, New Hebrides (now Vanuatu). These musical instruments consist of tree-trunks that have been hollowed out through a narrow longitudinal slit. In the past, they would have been installed at the edge of a clearing where the population congregated for the performance of ritual ceremonies. They would have been used to accompany singing and dancing.

Mastering and classifying material

The desire for classification is a relatively late phenomenon in advanced societies, although the ancient practices of India and China provide exceptions to the rule. Naming and inventorizing instruments, conceiving of them as being equivalent to members of a social group, is made possible only with the benefit of historical perspective.

Clearly the method will be different, depending on whether one is dealing with a culture based on writing or one based on an oral tradition. In the one case, consultation of written records and cross-referring of documentary evidence permits a comparative classification; in the other, the result of assembling oral data as reported by Christian missionaries or in anthropological field studies falls a long way short of a comprehensive survey of the world, and in this situation there is no choice but to confine oneself to citing a limited number of examples, without claiming to extrapolate any underlying thought processes.

In the case of classification, one may choose to approach the material from a linguistic viewpoint and thus distinguish categories of instruments as belonging to the same family because their names show similarities – even if sometimes, in terms of a strict typology of instruments, very distant relationships indeed may result. Certain terms which were originally used only to describe the material, have come to designate instruments of a particular form and playing technique. Examples of this are: the *olifant* (a horn made of elephant ivory); the *avena*, a small reed instrument made from a stem of oats (*Avena sativa*); the lute, which takes its name from the Arabic *al'ud*, meaning simply 'wood'. As for the French term 'carillon', referring notionally to a set of four bells (*carré* = 'square'), it alluded to the number of bells played together and also describes the method of playing.

The names of instruments frequently suggest the sound they produce, in other words they are invented or introduced into the language through onomatopœic associations. This is true for example of the terms used to designate the conch trumpet in Oceania or the ubiquitous 'jew's harp' in eastern Asia. The terms used are as varied as the populations that employ them, but in all cases the local language reflects the sounds the people hear, and the way in which they translate them into words. Although such names emanate from very diverse languages and countries, the similarities between them are sometimes so great that one is inclined to believe that the sound of each instrument does indeed act as the common denominator in an almost universal terminology. Thus, cymbals are called *sil-sil* in Tibetan, *zil* in Turkish, *selsele* in Hebrew, *salasal* in Arabic. The drums played in pairs in Ghana, the former Gold Coast, are called *ntumpane*, in the Ivory Coast *atûmbra* or *timmbana* (clearly related to the Latin *tympanum* and Greek *tympanon*).

There are numerous other examples which one could cite, but the onomatopœic relationship masks many differences between the individual instruments both in respect of their origins and distribution and the sounds they make. For this reason, a complete inventory of names, even if it existed, could not be used as the sole basis for determining classification.

Among the old systems that are still in use, and that have influenced Western ideas, is the Indian encyclopaedia *Natya-Shastra* (first century AD), which adopts as its criterion for classification the physical properties of materials used – that is, whether they are solid, rigid or elastic – and the ways in which the air is caused to vibrate. Thus four categories of vibrating elements are to be distinguished: stringed instruments which are plucked (*tata vadhya*) and those played by friction (*bitata vadhya*); wind instruments (*sushira vadhya*), either hollow or pierced, i.e. tubes through which air is blown; membrane instruments (*avanaddha vadhya*), which are covered; and idiophones (*ghana vadhya*) which are made from solid or rigid materials that vibrate when subjected to various methods of playing.

Later, in the thirteenth century, the musical treatise *Sangita Ratnakara* established categories based on functional considerations: solo instruments (*sushka*), accompanying instruments (*gitanuga*), instruments used only to accompany dancing (*nrityanuga*), and instruments employed to accompany both dances and songs (*gita-nrityanuga*).

The system of inventorization based on materials that was introduced by the Chinese represented an instinctive attempt on the part of man to classify and bring under control the abundance of nature. According to this system, in every sphere of the living world all things correspond, intermesh and link up in a manner that has more to do with sympathetic association than with reality, having more to do with magic than with acoustics, embracing all the elements of creation, and obedient to a single law.

The eight categories of sound, reflecting the different timbres emitted by various types of materials, are: clay, stone, bamboo, wood, gourd, silk, skin and metal. This classification goes right back to the time of the emperor Shun (2233–2188 BC). More recent texts based on Zhou dynasty rituals (1066–771 BC) mention eight categories of instruments and only four types of materials that emit sound: stone, skin, bamboo and silk, identified with the cardinal points of the compass and the seasons.

Essentially the same now as when it was invented, the Chinese system of classification is based on the nature of sounds, their *qi*, which reflects the harmony or the imbalance of natural forces. These in turn were considered to have an influence on political power.

Caught as they were between the menace of floods and the threat of drought – both of which brought famine in their wake – the ancient Chinese were greatly preoccupied with the conditions that would ensure survival. That presumably accounts for their obsession with wind and water. If a particular timbre was a criterion of classification, this was not so much for reasons of its aesthetic effect as for the influence it was supposed to have on meteorological conditions. In the same way as the sounds of certain instruments were believed to attract divinities or ancestor spirits if used at the time of the sacrifices that were regularly offered up to them, so the *qi* manifested itself in the form of wind and was propagated through music, which descended from heaven or rose up towards it, and by doing so directly influenced climatic changes. It was necessary to control the winds in order to ensure the arrival of rain in its due season and to help the crops grow. The harmonization of active earthly forces with those of the heavens took place within the organic whole of a philosophy in which music fulfilled the role of intermediary. Looked at in this light, the constituent materials of musical instruments formed part of a system of correspondences controlled by human beings, who exercised their influence in ritual dances aligned with a magic square on which the four points of the compass are superimposed.

Opposite: Tibetan Buddhist monk playing the oboe *rgya-gling*. According to the system by which Tibetan instruments are classified, its sound belongs to the peaceful as opposed to the violent register.

Above: Side-blown horn made of an elephant's tusk, known as an *olifant*. This particular instrument may have been commissioned in the 16th or 17th century by Portuguese clients of the Sherbro or Bolom peoples of Sierra Leone. L. 73 cm (28³/₄ in.).

The distribution of sound

The winds are associated with sounds: corresponding to each point of the compass, therefore, is a material and a particular sound and instrument-type.

1 To north corresponds skin *ge* 革, represented by the drum *gu* 鼓

2 To north-east corresponds the calabash *pao* 匏, represented by the mouth-organ

sheng 笙

3 To east corresponds bamboo *zhú* 竹, represented by the flute *xiao* 簫

4 To south-east corresponds wood *mu* 木, represented by the mortar *zhu* 柷

and the scraper *yü* 敔

5 To south corresponds silk *si* 絲, represented by the zithers *qin* 琴

and *se* 瑟

6 To south-west corresponds the earth *tu* 土, represented by the vessel flute *xun* 壎

7 To west corresponds metal *jin* 金, represented by the bells *zhong* 鐘

8 To north-west corresponds stone *shi* 石, represented by the stone chimes *qing* 磬

Musicology and musicologists

There probably exist as many parameters of classification of instruments as there are peoples in the world. Instrumental function, repertoire, playing technique, physical properties, materials employed – suggestions for suitable methods of imposing at least a semblance of order on this vast, chaotic family of instruments at large have come from all quarters.

In Europe, at the end of the twelfth century, Johannes de Muris described stringed instruments as *tensibilia*, winds as *inflatibilia* and percussion as *percussibilia*, while a work by the German composer and writer Michael Praetorius (1571–1621), *Syntagma Musicum*, included a section entitled *De organigrafia* devoted to medieval instruments. We then have to leap ahead to the nineteenth century, 1863 to be exact, to the treatise written by the Belgian François-Auguste Gevaert, in which he introduced a four-part classification of instruments: strings, winds, membranes and autophones. The first two of these groups were subdivided according to the means by which they are set in vibration: in the case of stringed instruments, this may be by friction, plucking or striking, while wind instruments are classified according to their characteristic features – holes, reeds and mouthpiece. A distinction is made between those instruments having a fixed or an indeterminate pitch, and between the type of materials of which autophones and membranophones are made. This formulation opened the way for one of his compatriots, Victor Charles Mahillon, who in his *Catalogue descriptif sur les principes acoustiques* (1888) reverted to the ancient Indian system of classification which subdivided instruments into autophones, membranophones and aerophones.

Mahillon's theory was succeeded in 1914 by the system devised by Erich von Hornbostel and Curt Sachs, which still prevails today. Several new criteria were introduced: the method of playing in respect of idiophones (the new name applied to autophones) and membranophones; external morphology for chordophones; and characteristic functioning parts for aerophones.

In 1931, André Schaeffner, founder of the Département d'Organologie Musicale (later called the Département d'Ethnomusicologie) at the Musée de l'Homme in Paris, advanced his *Nouvelle Classification méthodique des instruments de musique*, which drew the distinction between instruments with a solid vibrating body and those which caused the air to vibrate, the former being subdivided into solid bodies not susceptible to tension (idiophones in the system formulated by Hornbostel and Sachs), flexible solid bodies (as in lamellaphones) and solid bodies susceptible to tension (chordophones and membranophones). Wind instruments were placed in two basic categories: those with which the air is in external contact (e.g. bull-roarers) and those having an internal cavity. The constant references made here to the materials used emphasize the similarity that exists between this approach to classification and the ancient Chinese system.

Other approaches since then have included that of Hans-Heinz Dräger (1948), based on the external appearance of

Preceding page: The so-called 'Emilie Bell', cast in the eighth century in honour of king Songduk, now preserved in the National Museum of Kyongju in South Korea. According to legend, a young girl was sacrificed as the molten metal was poured to make the bell.

Right: The workshop of the Japanese instrument maker Najedini, c. 1925. In the West, an apprenticeship in making musical instruments consists largely in the observation and imitation of more experienced craftsmen.

Double page overleaf: The quality of an instrument's sound depends as much on that of the instrument maker as it does on the ear of the player: (left) an instrument maker of Russian origin tests the resonance of a violin's sounding board; (right) the bow passes over the strings of a cello.

an instrument, the nature of the vibrating element and the playing technique – overall, very similar to the principles laid down by Hornbostel and Sachs. More recently (1971), John Burton and Jeremy Montagu devised an easy-to-use method of classification with simplified definitions. The musicological section ('Section Organologique') of the International Council of Museums (ICOM) is working on a project to harmonize the various systems already in existence in museums, the aim being to establish a common standard worldwide.

In 1962 the well-known French ethnologist Claude Lévi-Strauss stated in *La Pensée sauvage*: 'Classification of any kind is better than chaos.' Musical instruments have been no less subject than any other type of artefact to peremptory classification imposed by human reason as a means of establishing control and understanding. However, they remain infinitely varied in terms of their forms, as well as their methods of use and their acoustic capabilities. Classifications may be superimposed one on another, each reinterpreting the last, and so on *ad infinitum*, but nature remains unperturbed. It is all a game involving scientific computations which in no way affect the musical instruments or diminish their essential mystery.

The task of the instrument maker

Not only does the instrument maker have all the potential of the natural world at his disposal, but he is at the same time the inheritor of a vast store of practical experience built up over generations. Everywhere in the world, he provides the vital link between nature and the musician. He is the alchemist who breathes life into matter, it is he who intervenes between that matter and the person who will eventually coax tunes from it. It is he who has to invent the sounds in the first place, before they can be arranged to produce melodies. He deals with the materials in their raw state, manipulates, refines and adjusts them out of a concern for the eminently praiseworthy human endeavour of making music.

The instrument maker knows how to choose his materials, and can judge their qualities and defects. His special knowledge comes from years of practical experience gained form working directly with materials, learning how to approach them, how to manipulate them. What the instrument maker fashions with his hands, is a direct response to nature, which will be expressed in sound. The instrument he sculpts and assembles is a veritable work of art, something unique, inspired both by a respect for longstanding tradition and a concern for progress; it may represent the product of an approach to sound that verges at times on the experimental.

Sometimes too the instrument maker is like a sort of soul-doctor, who knows when to intervene and when not, in his treatment of a damaged instrument; his concern will be for its continuing ability to resonate, which is far more important than some more obvious defect of manufacture. Sometimes, to interfere with a damaged body could prove fatal to the sound of an instrument, which may still ring true despite the physical scar.

Construction, restoration, achieving an ideal balance of the elements of the instrument so as to obtain the best possible sound, these are the skills of the instrument maker. There can be few natural materials which he cannot exploit. The essential challenge is to adopt materials and use them for musical or decorative purposes, or if possible for both at once. The materials over which he exerts physical control (in contrast to the musicologist, who aims to control them intellectually by listing all their properties) may be human, animal, vegetable or mineral in origin, and are so varied that it would be impossible to list them all.

Opposite: The coats of varnish or resin applied to the violin are crucial in determining the instrument's quality of sound. Seen here is a violin maker from Cremona, the Italian town famous for its makers of stringed instruments, among them Stradivarius.

Above: A violin under construction in the maker's workshop.

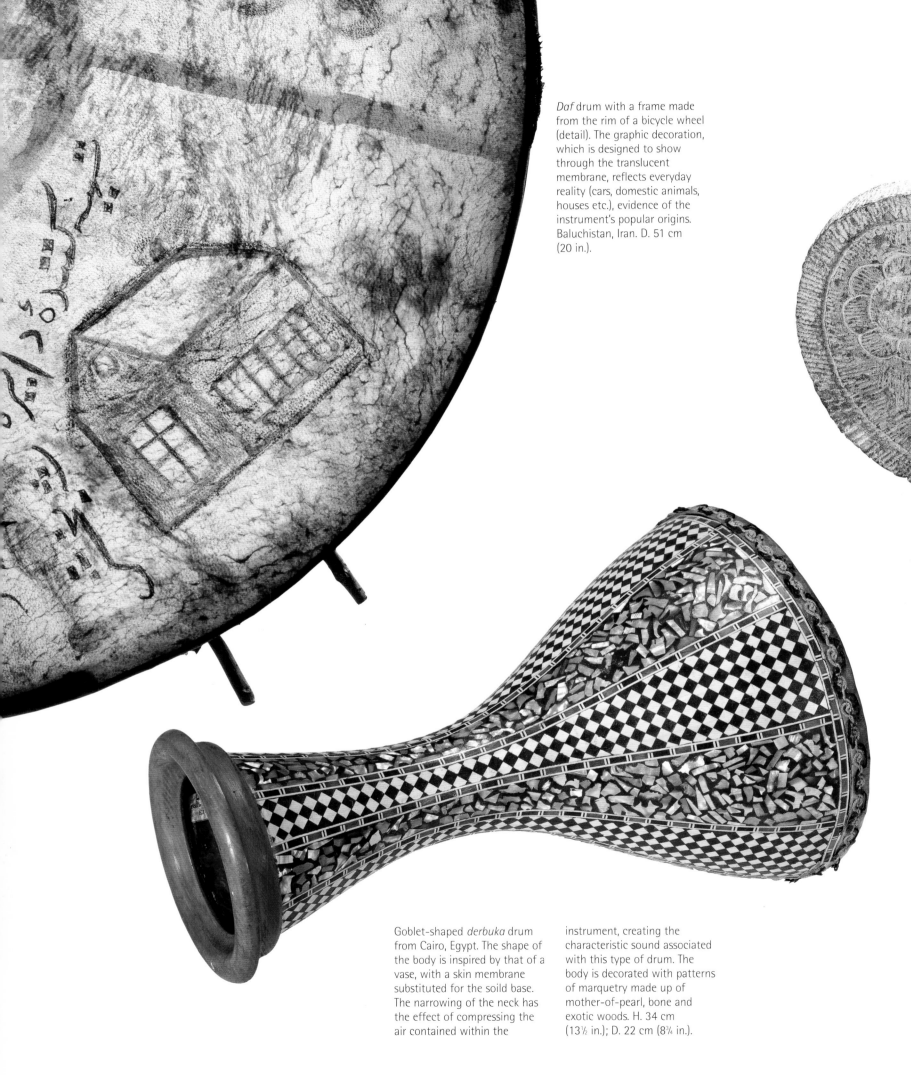

Daf drum with a frame made from the rim of a bicycle wheel (detail). The graphic decoration, which is designed to show through the translucent membrane, reflects everyday reality (cars, domestic animals, houses etc.), evidence of the instrument's popular origins. Baluchistan, Iran. D. 51 cm (20 in.).

Goblet-shaped *derbuka* drum from Cairo, Egypt. The shape of the body is inspired by that of a vase, with a skin membrane substituted for the soild base. The narrowing of the neck has the effect of compressing the air contained within the instrument, creating the characteristic sound associated with this type of drum. The body is decorated with patterns of marquetry made up of mother-of-pearl, bone and exotic woods. H. 34 cm (13½ in.); D. 22 cm (8¾ in.).

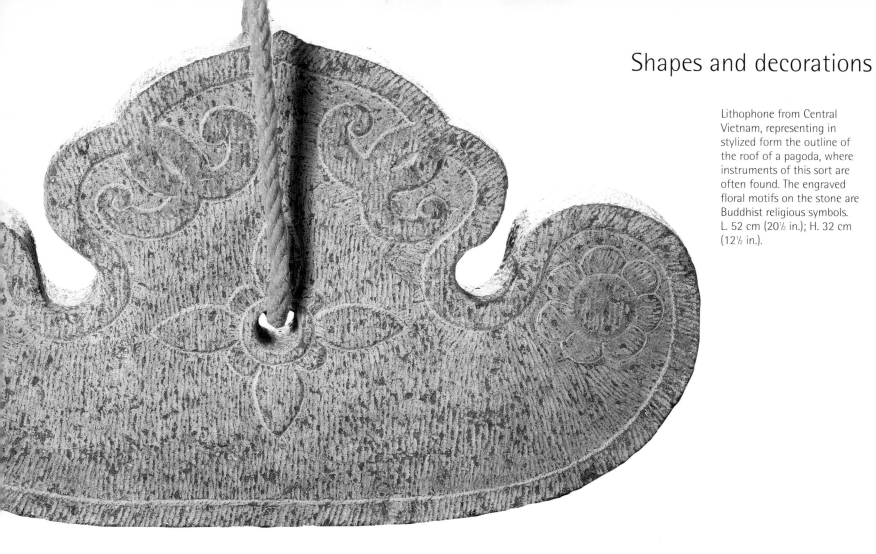

Lithophone from Central Vietnam, representing in stylized form the outline of the roof of a pagoda, where instruments of this sort are often found. The engraved floral motifs on the stone are Buddhist religious symbols. L. 52 cm (20½ in.); H. 32 cm (12½ in.).

Santur board zither with resonator and seventy-two metal strings, from Qazvin in Iran. The instrument, in the shape of a parallelogram, is decorated overall with paintings of musicians and dancers. It is played as part of an ensemble that includes a *kemanche* fiddle and *târ* lute decorated by the same artist. L. of sides 35 and 90 cm (13¾ and 35½ in.).

In the forests of southern Chad, the hunters of *kudu* antelope participate before their departure in a ritual incorporating the playing of this side-blown instrument made from the spiral horn of their quarry.

Right: *Ganga* drum played by the Gwana of the Essaouira region of Morocco. The richly decorated membrane is made of animal skin, probably that of a goat.

Bodily sacrifices

Human and animal body parts are often very similar in configuration, hence in practical terms the one can be used in place of the other. Whether we are concerned with skin, bone, teeth, hair, feathers, horn, fur or entrails, to mention only some of the parts that can be put to use, both man and beast have been subject to large-scale plundering of their bodies living or dead, in order that musical instruments may be created from them.

The membranes used to cover the frame of a drum or in chordophones, specifically lutes, may be derived from the pericardium (the sac surrounding the heart) of a calf, which is thin and has good resonating properties. Similarly, snakeskin may be used for lyres, sharkskin for rattles, whiplashes, thongs and the sticks used to beat the timpani. Bagpipes, wherever they occur, have an airtight reservoir made from animal skin which is inflated as the piper blows into it; and in the days of the Inca empire, drums were frequently covered with the skin of defeated enemies who had been flayed alive.

Bones were used in the making of some of the most ancient instruments known to man. These include the phalanxes of reindeer and other hunted animals (from which prehistoric man made whistles and scrapers), as well as the bones of large birds such as the common crane. The ulnae of wading birds, vultures and eagles have been used to make transverse flutes ever since the Upper Palaeolithic, as is demonstrated by the finds at Isturitz, at the cave of Le Placard and at Peyrat in France, as well as at other prehistoric sites, including Molodova in Western Ukraine. The practice continues today among North American Indian tribes and in Central Asia.

Snake vertebrae are sometimes used as small bells or chimes, being threaded onto a network of strings which is attached to a rattle made from a gourd that is itself filled with seeds – a type employed in initiation rites in the former Dahomey in West Africa. A similar sort of string netting threaded with human vertebrae is incorporated into the traditional magical garment worn as an apron by the Tibetan shaman.

Fish vertebrae strung on a cord are used in Norway to make a whizzer or thunderstick. The 'humming bone' of European popular tradition was, however, artificially perforated, as is seen in the prehistoric bull-roarers from Saint-Marcel (Indre) and at Laugerie-Basse (Dordogne), which date from the Magdalenian era (see chapter 1). Archaeological finds made at Skania in Sweden and at Kongemosen in Denmark, the latter dating from the Mesolithic, show that this type of instrument was also in use among the Vikings. Bone scrapers were employed in large numbers in Siberia in the Palaeolithic era, and are also found in the Americas.

A series of animal rib-bones may be laid out side by side to form a sort of xylophone which is struck with sticks. Whale ribs are used by the Inuit peoples to form the frames of drums.

The human skull is the main constituent of the Tibetan rattle drum, the *damaru*, which consists of two joined crania

Hollow bodies

Kundu hourglass drum (detail) from New Guinea. Its carrying-handle is carved in the form of a crocodile, founder of the cosmos according to the myths of many Oceanic peoples. The upper part of the animal's body is visible on the right. The membrane covering the head of the drum is the skin of an iguana. L. 50 cm (19¾ in.); D. 14 cm (5½ in.).

Hatun charango lute with five double strings. This is one of several hybrid musical instruments found in the Andes as a result of contacts between European and native cultures. The instrument has the general shape of a small Spanish guitar, while its soundbox consists of the carapace of an armadillo. Chuquisaca, Bolivia. L. 98 cm (38½ in.).

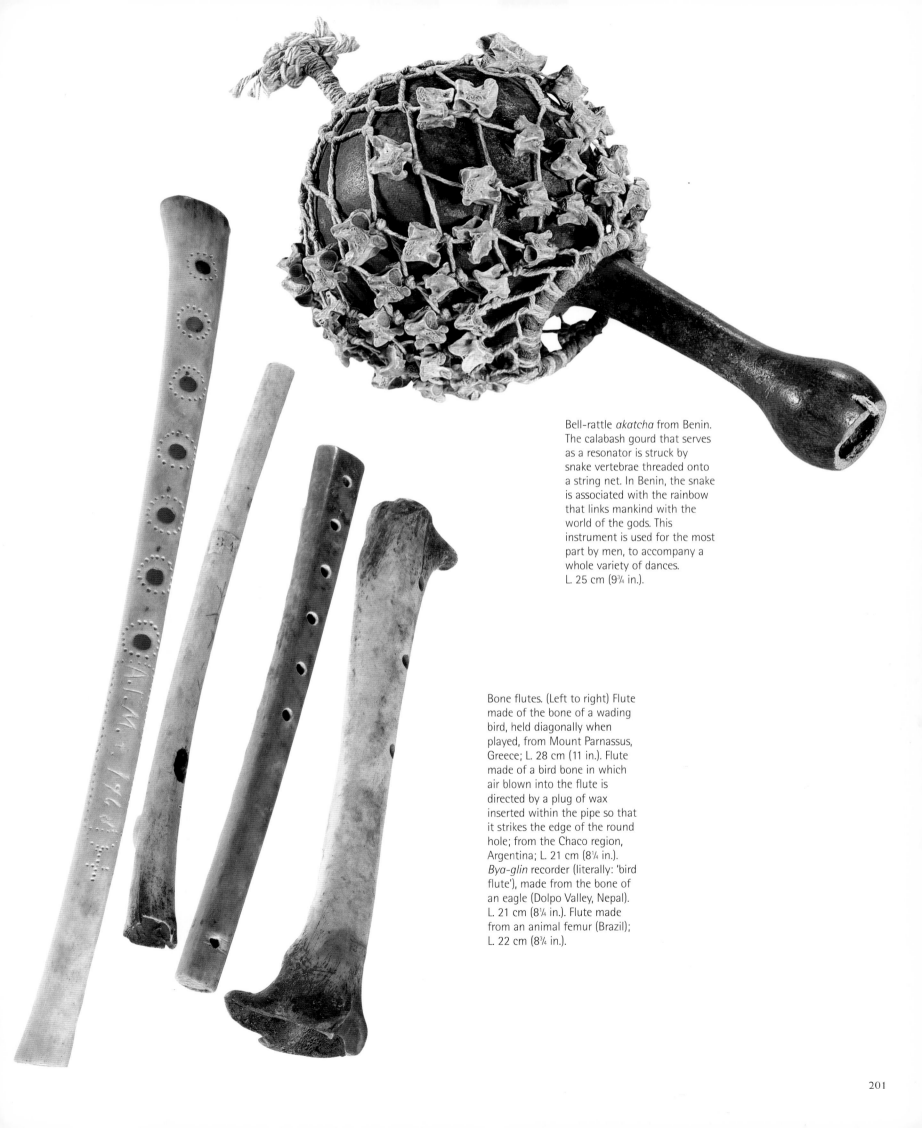

Bell-rattle *akatcha* from Benin. The calabash gourd that serves as a resonator is struck by snake vertebrae threaded onto a string net. In Benin, the snake is associated with the rainbow that links mankind with the world of the gods. This instrument is used for the most part by men, to accompany a whole variety of dances. L. 25 cm (9¾ in.).

Bone flutes. (Left to right) Flute made of the bone of a wading bird, held diagonally when played, from Mount Parnassus, Greece; L. 28 cm (11 in.). Flute made of a bird bone in which air blown into the flute is directed by a plug of wax inserted within the pipe so that it strikes the edge of the round hole; from the Chaco region, Argentina; L. 21 cm (8¼ in.). *Bya-glin* recorder (literally: 'bird flute'), made from the bone of an eagle (Dolpo Valley, Nepal). L. 21 cm (8¼ in.). Flute made from an animal femur (Brazil); L. 22 cm (8¾ in.).

with skin stretched across the open sides. Human femurs used as trumpets are traditionally sounded by Buddhist priests during religious ceremonies, as well as by shamans and pilgrims moving from one monastery to the next. This practice is also found in cultures in both Central Asia and America, the difference being that the bones are those of large mammals, such as the jaguar or stag.

In Guatemala, the Lacandón Indians, who hunt monkeys for food, use the animals' skulls as rattles. Bones are also put to practical use, strung together to make a kind of aeolian harp or wind chime.

Of horn and ivory

Animal horns, depending on their size, can serve as whistles, flutes or pipes, or – in the case of the very largest kinds – as a kind of trumpet or megaphone. Sometimes the horn of one animal is inserted into that of another, as in the Peruvian telescopic horn. The horns of some of the *cervidae* are used as hunting horns or instruments of summons in religious ceremonies, and may be either end-blown or side-blown. A prime example is the ram's horn (Hebrew, *shofar*), blown during Jewish rituals.

Animal horns are also used as resonators for xylophones, in combination with gourds of comparable size. Bull-roarers made of reindeer antlers from the Magdalenian era were found at La Roche near Lalinde, in the Dordogne. These are decorated with red ochre and engraved with stripes in exactly the same manner as those still produced today by Australian aborigines. Some horns feature a pattern of natural grooves, like those of a breed of pygmy sheep (*Ovis ammonaries*) found in Cameroun, and these lend themselves naturally to being scraped with a stick.

In the Palaeolithic era, teeth were combined with small pieces of bone to make acoustic ornaments, often worn as pendants, as evidenced in northern Spain: at Cueva Aizbitarte, shark's teeth were used, and in Cueva Bolin Koba, stag's teeth. An acoustic bracelet dating from the Palaeolithic era and made of mammoth ivory was found at Mezin in Ukraine. In the eastern regions of Siberia, walrus tusks were used to make idioglot jew's harps. Elephant ivory provided the material in ancient Egypt for clappers, carved in the shape of hands and forearms, which were beaten one against the other; the later clappers called *tengere*, which were modelled on them, were made of wood. On the African continent, there are innumerable examples of horns made of ivory, many of them side-blown; these tend to change in colour as they age, from white to dark brown. Until quite recently, ivory was the standard material used for white piano keys.

Both ivory and horn are materials frequently employed for parts of stringed instruments, such as nuts of violin bows, fixed or movable bridges, frets, pegs and a variety of ornamental features.

Strung together in a cluster, the beaks of birds are used as chimes, as are the hooves of stags and the ears of gazelles, among the Bushmen of Botswana and Zambia. The spines of the sea urchin *Heterocentrotus mammilatus* also serve the same purpose among some of the native peoples of the Philippines.

Tortoiseshells used in various musical instruments are a familiar sight. These may be used either for simple indirect percussion, as in the friction idiophone of the Amazonian Indians, or struck, as among the Lacandon of Mexico and Venezuela. In old Mayan paintings musicians are depicted striking a tortoiseshell with a forked stick. A tortoiseshell may also be used as a leg-plate or a rattle, for example in shamanistic practices among North American Indians.

Tortoiseshells are also adapted as readymade soundboxes for a number of chordophones, notably Egyptian lyres and certain lutes in use among the white populations of Africa. The carapace of the armadillo can also serve as a resonance chamber, as seen in lutes of the *charango* type in South America.

Below: Egyptian *tânbura* lyre whose soundbox consists of a tortoiseshell. The seven strings are made of animal gut and stretched between a bamboo cane crossbar or 'yoke' and a sounding board of animal skin. H. 58 cm (22¾ in.).

Opposite: Sound-making toy called *trek-tre*. The Joraï children of Vietnam amuse themselves by passing a thin wooden stick rapidly between two shells attached to the ends of a split bamboo cane: the shells collide and make a sound like the clashing of small cymbals.

Conches and shells

From the earliest times man has used shells for musical purposes, selecting and arranging them in a variety of ways: piercing and threading them together as necklaces; hanging them in the wind to act as chimes or on the body as tinkling ornaments; using cords made from leather, vegetable material or bark; or suspending them on sticks to form rattles. Bivalves are ideally suited to become castanets or crotalums, and the grooved external surfaces of certain shells lend themselves to being used as scrapers, as is the case with the *Cardium*, while yet others may be transformed into whizzers or thundersticks. Fragments of shell strung onto sticks, either forked or made into rings, form the sistra in use among Malaysian fishermen.

Conches and other shells have been adapted for use as whistles, megaphones and trumpets in many areas of the world, from South-East Asia to Madagascar, in India and Tibet, in the Pacific region and in the Americas.

Mother-of-pearl decorates many musical instruments, in particular lutes and zithers, where the contours of the soundboard and the rose (in the case of an instrument having a sound hole in the box) bear ornamental friezes or marquetry motifs embellished with mother-of-pearl.

Double page overleaf: Prayer flags on the Himalayan mountains outside temples and villages. The rustling of the fabric in the wind is believed to indicate the presence of benevolent spirits.

Feathers, horsehair and human hair

Various types of feather, which by their very nature incorporate a narrow tube, are used by North American Indian and Arctic Inuit peoples as whistles, and there are also examples of pan-pipes made from condor feathers. Feathers, if cut to a point, may also be employed as quill plectrums for harpsichord jacks. In addition, feathers are used as decorative elements on a variety of instruments, notably gourd whistles, on end-blown horns in South America and *bororo* bull-roarers.

Horse hair and human hair, coated with resin, are used in the manufacture of bows, lute and fiddle strings, and for various other items like the cords of friction drums. They can also be plaited to form carrying-handles and ornaments for musical instruments.

The cocoon is another material resource used, directly or indirectly, for musical purposes. Thus, some kinds may be used as chimes, while others, as in the case of cocoons woven by spiders, may serve as the vibrating element of the African *balafon*, or else as aerophones.

Silk, formerly used in Asia for chordophones (zithers, lutes or fiddles) is now rarely employed; the soft sound produced by silken strings was a prized attribute of the Chinese zither *guqin*.

The orchestra of plants

The variety of vegetable materials that can be exploited and put to musical uses is immense. Rattles, whistles, body chimes, percussion idiophones, free aerophones and scrapers are all derived from the husks of dried fruits and the seed-pods of flowers, such as the opium poppy (*Papaver somniferum*) or the pomegranate (*Punica granatum*); larger types include the beak-shaped seeds of the saman tree (*Samanea saman*), the rattle/amulet much prized by the Thai people, or the giant seed-pods of *Delonix regia* of South America, the ridged inside surface of which makes an excellent scraper.

Acoustic costumes that accompany dancing performed in celebration of tree cults are made from the large leaves of *Magnolia grandiflora*, which create sound effects resembling the murmuring or gurgling of water. Rain sticks, in the form

The Indian *sitar* incorporates both metal and gut strings. The difference in texture and elasticity between the two materials gives the strings distinctive acoustic qualities, providing the instrument with its unique sound. This is further enhanced by the vibrations of a set of sympathetic metal strings stretched below the frets.

of bamboo canes partially filled with cactus spines, may be turned upside down or shaken to imitate the sound of running water.

Among naturally occurring rattles, the dried calabash or bottle gourd (*Lagenaria siceraria*) produces a rather deep sound, while the pomegranate is altogether lighter in tone, and the mass of tiny seeds inside a dried poppyhead make a high-pitched noise.

Various kinds of whistle are created out of acorn cups and dried fruit stones, those of plums or cherries being used for ultrasonic whistles. Very high-pitched sounds are produced by apricot and peach stones, as well as by hazelnuts, almonds and walnuts already pierced by the teeth of dormice or squirrels and the beaks of birds. Larger exotic fruits such as *Lucuma mammosa* used by the Amazonian Indians, or *Oncoba spinosa* from Africa, emit a deeper sound. If hollow materials are perforated with several holes, they are classified as ocarinas.

Branches of trees hung with fruit or panicles of seeds, such as those of *Paulownia tomentosa*, produce a sound like leaves quivering in the wind, traditionally revered as the voice of the gods, while bamboo leaves and sections of bamboo canes of various thicknesses will, if shaken together, emit sounds in different pitches.

Gourds, rushes and bamboos may be marked with grooves and then scraped, above a gourd that acts as a resonator, with the aid of a plant spine or a stick, which may be made from a variety of different materials.

Willow and other natural fibres are used for constructing rattles of all shapes and kinds, as well as in accessories such as the supports for the small gongs used in China in *nanguan* music, for the outer sheaths of pottery drums in Benin, the handles of lutes, or the plaited *tapas* wrapped around drums in Oceania. Another special item is a plaited straw helmet worn by players of the *shakuhachi*, the Japanese end-blown notched flute; this isolates the musician from the outside world and at the same time functions as a resonator, producing microtones. Some of the *maracas* used in South America are made of plaited vegetable fibres.

Strings made of rushes, couch grass or raffia are stretched above bark-lined cavities to form the clay zithers made in the ground in parts of Asia and Africa. In Madagascar and Vietnam, such cords may be as much as 4 metres (13 ft) in length. Fibres of this kind also form the tautened string and vibrating element of the primitive musical bow made from a single bamboo cane, and they are also employed for the strings of the majority of the African chordophones, harps and pluriarcs.

Above: Whistles with a blowing hole and two smaller holes used to modify the sound, made from small calabash gourds. Kraho Amerindians, Goiás state, Brazil. L. 6 and 8 cm (2¼ and 3¼ in.).

Overleaf: Horn played by the Masa of southern Chad. The instrument consists of two calabash gourds of different shapes. The long thin gourd forms the main part of the instrument, in the sense that this is where the fingerholes are situated, while the round gourd functions as the bell of the horn, in which the sound circulates and its timbre is transformed.

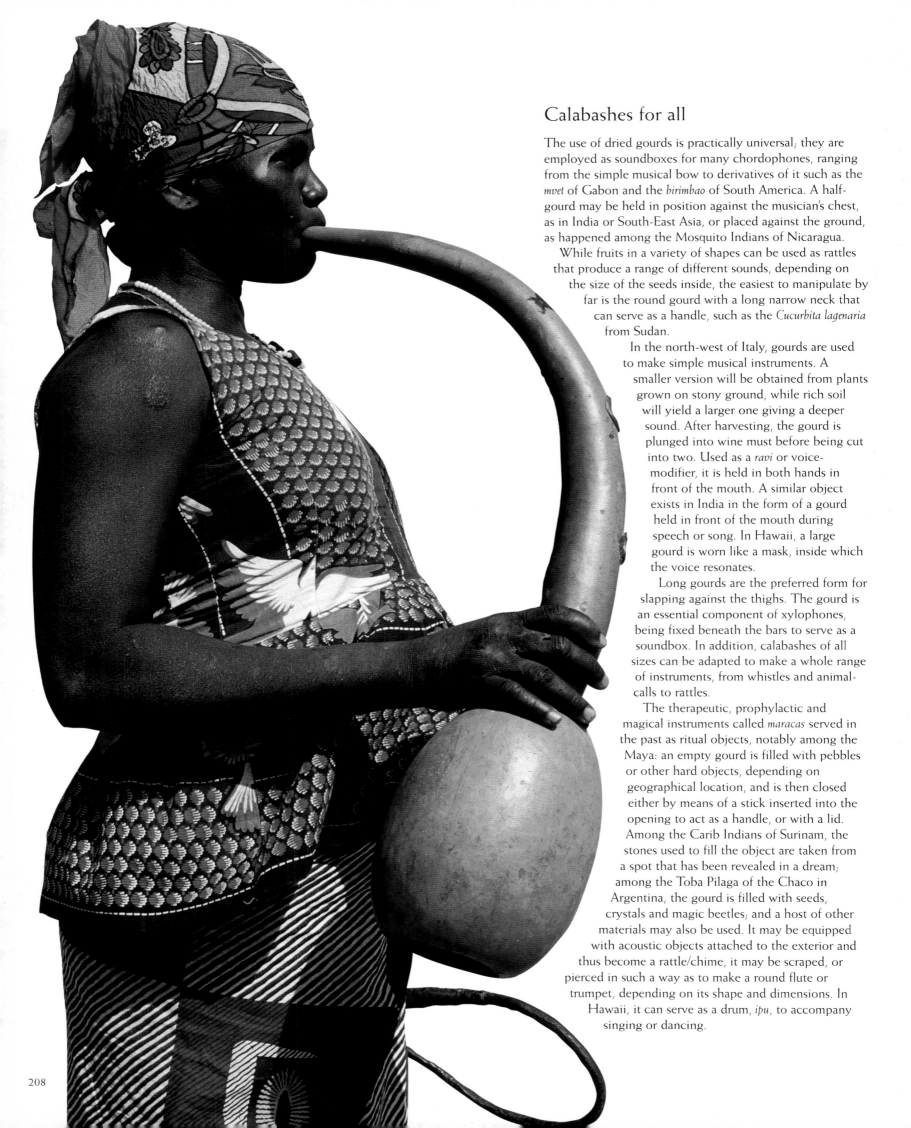

Calabashes for all

The use of dried gourds is practically universal; they are employed as soundboxes for many chordophones, ranging from the simple musical bow to derivatives of it such as the *mvet* of Gabon and the *birimbao* of South America. A half-gourd may be held in position against the musician's chest, as in India or South-East Asia, or placed against the ground, as happened among the Mosquito Indians of Nicaragua.

While fruits in a variety of shapes can be used as rattles that produce a range of different sounds, depending on the size of the seeds inside, the easiest to manipulate by far is the round gourd with a long narrow neck that can serve as a handle, such as the *Cucurbita lagenaria* from Sudan.

In the north-west of Italy, gourds are used to make simple musical instruments. A smaller version will be obtained from plants grown on stony ground, while rich soil will yield a larger one giving a deeper sound. After harvesting, the gourd is plunged into wine must before being cut into two. Used as a *ravi* or voice-modifier, it is held in both hands in front of the mouth. A similar object exists in India in the form of a gourd held in front of the mouth during speech or song. In Hawaii, a large gourd is worn like a mask, inside which the voice resonates.

Long gourds are the preferred form for slapping against the thighs. The gourd is an essential component of xylophones, being fixed beneath the bars to serve as a soundbox. In addition, calabashes of all sizes can be adapted to make a whole range of instruments, from whistles and animal-calls to rattles.

The therapeutic, prophylactic and magical instruments called *maracas* served in the past as ritual objects, notably among the Maya: an empty gourd is filled with pebbles or other hard objects, depending on geographical location, and is then closed either by means of a stick inserted into the opening to act as a handle, or with a lid. Among the Carib Indians of Surinam, the stones used to fill the object are taken from a spot that has been revealed in a dream; among the Toba Pilaga of the Chaco in Argentina, the gourd is filled with seeds, crystals and magic beetles; and a host of other materials may also be used. It may be equipped with acoustic objects attached to the exterior and thus become a rattle/chime, it may be scraped, or pierced in such a way as to make a round flute or trumpet, depending on its shape and dimensions. In Hawaii, it can serve as a drum, *ipu*, to accompany singing or dancing.

A polymorphous utensil and musical instrument, the hollow calabash can also be struck in various different ways, depending on the shapes of the gourds themselves: for example, it may be struck on the side where the orifice is situated, as in the Pacific region, or by means of compressed air (in the same manner as Neolithic peoples used earthenware vessels) or on the base, as with the Fulani peoples of Mauritania and Mali, where the player sits holding the instrument pressed against his thighs or stands holding it against his abdomen.

As a soundbox for chordophones, the calabash gourd is sometimes replaced by a coconut, if something of smaller dimension is required; it may also be used as a half-shell, for rubbing a surface or striking against water. In Africa and among the Yaquis Indians in Mexico is found a type of water drum made of a half-gourd which, when floating on water, is beaten either with the fingers or with a stick; several half-gourds of different sizes may be played together, polyrhythmically and polyphonically.

Finally, the calabash may be cut into sets of double discs, which are then threaded onto a forked stick to make a sistrum. The discs can be of different shapes, depending on the diameter of the calabash, and may have notched edges.

The bamboo tradition

Bamboo canes and reeds have made an incalculable contribution to the manufacture of musical instruments, such that it would be quite impossible to list all the

instruments made from these two plant types, or that contain some part of them.

Cane is the ideal material for the vibrating strips or single reeds of the type most familiar to us from the ubiquitous jew's harp, which is distributed all over Asia, in the Philippines and New Guinea. In this common instrument, which uses the oral cavity as the resonator, the tongue or blade may be integral with the frame (idioglot) or not, and there may be as many as five inserted metal tongues (as in the type used by the Atayal of Taiwan). The same principle applies to clarinets, whether the reed is single and idioglot, as among the Gaojiro Indians of South America, or whether it is of the type known as 'beating', and is inserted in the top of the pipe, in the player's mouth or in the lower section of the pipe. Clarinets may be double-pipe, consisting of two reed tubes, as in the case of the *urua* of the Camayura Indians of Brazil, and may also have a resonator such as a gourd, like the *pungi* employed by Indian snake-charmers. In China and South-East Asia, the tradition of the mouth-organ made from bamboo goes back a thousand years. The instrument exhibits many variations, it may or may not have a soundbox, and the bamboo pipes may be arranged in a bundle or laid flat in the manner of a raft. An early prototype of the oboe exists in the form of the Armenian *duduk*, for example, which is played by directing the breath between two blades made of dried reed, which are bound together and adjusted before being inserted into the pipe.

The original underlying principle of both the musical bow and the hunting bow is that a bamboo cane is made to form an arc under tension from a string. This was the basis for a long line of chordophones, in which wood eventually took over from bamboo as it offered a more rigid material for sticks and the soundboxes of zithers and lutes. Only in the case of the tube zither does bamboo continue to be used: here, the soundbox consists of in internodal section of cane closed at each end by the naturally occurring joints, while the idioglot strings are formed of strips of bark raised up onto small bridges; the zither may either be struck or played with a plectrum. Derivative forms are the *phin* of South-East Asia and the Madagascan *valiha*.

In South-East Asia, the Philippines and the Pacific region, many native peoples employ a split bamboo cane as a percussive idiophone, generally held in one hand and struck against the opposite forearm. A bamboo cane about the length of a fishing rod may be used as a whip, which is caused to vibrate and emit sound by sharp flicks of the wrist. Bamboo canes may be suspended horizontally, either whole or cut along their length, so as to form a sort of xylophone, as found in South-East Asia. Sections of bamboo of varying in length and diameter are used as pestles to crush grain, either on the ground or against a stone slab placed over a ditch that serves as a resonance chamber, or in a mortar. When several are used simultaneously, as happens in South-East Asia, the result is a contrapuntal polyrhythm and polyphony. Single bamboo canes are also used as rhythm sticks in many parts of the world, including Polynesia and the Amazon Basin.

Chimes may be made by the use of small pieces of bamboo of different lengths suspended from a horizontal bar, while a bundle of dried bamboo canes will produce a soft metallic sound when shaken. Marked with grooves, a piece of bamboo makes an excellent scraper. Filled with small seeds, the hollow tube becomes a rattle.

The *angklung*, widespread in Indonesia and the Pacific region, is a bamboo rattle made of graded sections inserted vertically into slits in a horizontal cane. The instrument must normally be used with other such rattles to produce polyphonic sound.

The slits and holes that occur naturally in bamboo stems can produce whistling noises when the wind blows. Certain peoples attempt to recreate that magical sound by cutting canes with such perforations; a group consisting of canes of differing heights is then planted in a windy spot so as to form a bamboo organ, used largely on ritual occasions, e.g. in the Solomon Islands. In China, aeolian flutes made of bamboo are attached to decorative kites, so that the flying image will be accompanied by sounds. If cane is used to make a bull-roarer, this will be rectangular in shape, following the direction of the fibres (Indonesia). From the simple technique of cutting reeds and bamboo canes of various sizes to make whistles with different sounds (New Guinea), developed the idea of aligning them, resulting in the bamboo syrinx or pan-pipes as found in China. This was also how the intervals of the musical scale were discovered.

Bamboo cane is one of the principal materials used for wind instruments, and may be end-blown or side-blown, the aperture in the latter case being cut in a variety of different shapes – square, round, rectangular or oval. In the case of bamboo flutes the principal variations centre on the type of orifice that forms the mouthpiece. If this is 'open', the flute will be held obliquely (as with the *nay* in the Arab world), with the mouth partially covering the orifice; the rim may also be bevelled if the bamboo stem is thick; notched flutes are held vertically (as with the Chinese *xiao* or the Andean *quena*); if the flute is of the transverse type, the hole is made in the side of a cane stopped at both ends (Shuara Indians, Amazonia). Orifices with a plug or block are characteristic of an end-blown flute having, on the lower surface, a window which causes the air inside the pipe to vibrate: this is the *flauto dolce*, *Blockflöte* or recorder of the Western world. In the case of the nose flute used in South-East Asia, Oceania and South America, the blowing orifice is pierced close to the stopped end of the pipe.

Wood and bark

Wood and bark are essential constituents of a vast number of instruments. Hollow tree-trunks were originally used as drums while still standing. Subsequently trees were cut or slit in such a way as to produce the specific sounds desired, and such drums occur in a variety of shapes and sizes. Ultimately the wooden drum was transmuted into the body of the membrane drum.

When sawn into small pieces, the tree-trunk can be put to innumerable uses: as strips of varying length for the bars of a xylophone; in the *tsalaparta* of the Basque country; for castanets of various kinds; as clappers, etc. Transformed into a free aerophone, in the form of a flat sculpted blade decorated with engraved or painted geometric motifs, a suitable piece of timber becomes a bull-roarer. Wood is also ideal for the soundbox of all the different types of chordophone, from the zither to the lute, the psaltery to the harpsichord, the violin to the guitar.

Scraper from Madagascar. A blade of bamboo is split so as to form a brush made of thin strips, and this is used to scrape grooves made on the surface of a bamboo cane.

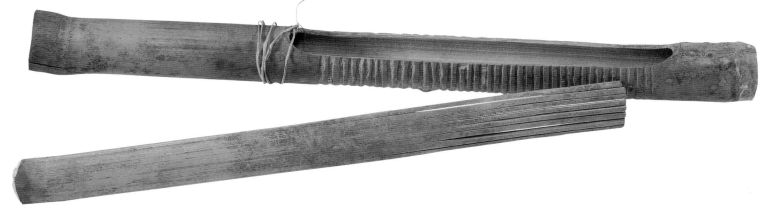

Making pan-pipes.
The 'Aré'Aré of the Solomon Islands.

After choosing the bamboo canes and stripping off their leaves, the musician determines the length of each pipe by reference to an existing instrument. Comparing the sound emitted by a newly cut pipe with the corresponding

The drum maker starts by cutting the wood for the body of the drum, which consists of an urn-shaped upper section and a base. After hollowing out both parts, an antelope skin from which the hair has been removed is stretched over the larger aperture and kept taut by strips of leather. Small wooden wedges are inserted between the lacing and the body wall, allowing the tension to be adjusted.

Clay, stone and metal

The earth on which we tread has provided the basis of some of the oldest instruments known to man, such as clay bells, whistles and prehistoric rattles filled with small stones. The pre-Columbian Amerindian civilizations in particular produced a variety of vessel flutes, compound pipes and wind instruments.

Utensils as well as musical instruments, the pot-drums of Benin were used for percussion as were certain other round pots in India, and similarly earthenware vessels were used as resonators during singing. In the case of pottery vessels used as timpani, notably the shells of such drums as the Moroccan *derbuka*, baked clay gives a particularly rich and soft resonance, though the instruments are by their nature very fragile.

When the first lithophones were developed in prehistoric times, stones were either struck individually or arranged in rows, according to size, in such a manner as to form a scale or to allow tunes to be played. The stones originally rubbed together to make fire became musical instruments, as seen in the stone castanets of India. Flat or round waterworn stones from places such as river banks, or pebbles from the seashore, were chosen for their hardness and the quality of the ringing sound they produced when banged together. In Hawaii, pieces of the local lava (called *ili-ili*) are used as an accompaniment to dancing; they may also be rubbed or scraped. Stone bull-roarers are much rarer, because of their weight; among the known examples are stones with incised

decoration or which have been incised and shaped in such a way as to produce a particular sound. Stone whistles and compound pipes are among the oldest musical instruments.

Certain stalactites and stalagmites make natural gongs; the vibrations produced by percussion cause sound waves to travel along 'pipes' created by erosion. Formations such as that in the Bassura cave, at Toirano in Liguria, are known as stone organs, because each of the column-like blades, when struck with a wooden paddle, emits a different note; these resemble the pure sound produced by woodwind or bamboo instruments. There is also evidence for the practice of striking stalactites in Java, in the so-called Gamelan cave.

Metal has long been a favoured material for the manufacture of musical instruments as it can be subjected to considerable bending without the risk of fracturing. Gold, silver and copper were in use in prehistoric times, iron was introduced during the first millennium BC, and after that tin, lead and mercury – all of them solid, hard, bright and shiny elements capable of producing a good sound.

Man learned to use metals in their pure state and in alloys, exploiting their ability to melt when heated and to solidify on cooling. Sophisticated workmanship and the durability of the resulting products placed metal in a special situation, and gave the blacksmith and others who handled it a social prestige that was enhanced by a sense of mystery and awe. Metal can be used to recreate forms previously perfected in other materials and, because the resulting sounds are so different, their use can also be adapted. Metallurgy opened up infinite possibilities: man could regard himself as the master of nature, capable of creating with his technological expertise objects that would live on beyond him, not only as musical instruments but as material evidence of his civilization. Perhaps the obvious example of such survivals is the bell, which has always been associated with the imposing timbre of cast iron or bronze. However, most of the idiophones are involved in this historical process, whether in the form of rattles, rhythm sticks, body chimes, bells or sistra made of iron, plaques of iron or bronze (alone or in a group) struck with a mallet, cymbals, bowls, copper gongs, telescopic or one-piece horns, lamellaphones made of gongs or plaques. In addition to all these and other instruments, metal is used to make a variety of instrumental parts, such as the shells of drums, the bells of oboes, organ pipes, etc.

This selective inventory of materials would be incomplete without some reference to a whole new class of instruments in use today, the found and reclaimed objects utilizing cast-off artefacts. Should we really be so surprised that at the dawn of the third millennium bull-roarers can be made of plastic piping and rattles of sprinkler heads, that drum frames are made out of bicycle wheels, and lutes and fiddles adapted from old jerry-cans? Far from regarding this extraordinary list as symptomatic of the decadence of Western civilizations, it is possible on the contrary to interpret such creativity as a mark of man's unquenchable inventiveness for, although the sounds themselves may change very little, people continue, everywhere and always, to make music. Even if cut off from the source of its original materials, that tradition will continue uninterrupted.

Below: The lithophone *picancala*, used by the Kabiye of Togo. Five basalt rocks are arranged in the form of a star on a bed of straw and beaten with two small stones. The melodic line is carried by the right hand, which moves to and fro between the four stones situated on either side of the musician. The fifth, which is much larger and produces the deepest sound, is struck only by the left hand, which sets up a rhythmic accompaniment to the melody.

Opposite A: Young musician from Maseru in Lesotho. The ingenuity with which cast-off materials such as oil cans are adapted and transformed into musical instruments offers proof of the strength of the attachment musicians feel for their musical heritage.

Kalali lute (detail) made by the Teda people, in the region of Fezzen in Libya. The resonance chamber consists of an enamelled metal container that was originally a kitchen utensil, and the two strings are made of fishing line. These manufactured elements are combined with natural materials like chamois skin and the branch of a date palm, used respectively for the sound table and neck of the instrument. L. 21 cm (8¼ in.).

Pair of rattles from the Democratic Republic of Congo, made of soldered and pierced sheet metal. Being both solid and malleable, pieces of sheet metal that can be salvaged outside factories can be given a new lease of life by musicians. L. 24 cm (9½ in.).

Instruments made from recycled junk

Double flute made by Rawaut shepherds of Madhya Pradesh, India. Purely from the point of view of acoustics, pipes made of synthetic materials, being more homogenous and rigid than either bamboo canes or reeds, are ideally suited for the manufacture of flutes. The flautist blows down both tubes at once, using the technique of circular breathing. He plays the melodic line on the pipe with five fingerholes, while maintaining a drone on the other one. L. 53 cm (20¾ in.).

Gidiga lamellaphone with five plucked metal tongues, made by the Hausa people of the Tahoua region of Niger. The body of the instrument consists of a salvaged metal can with a piece of wood inserted to form a sounding board. In its original version, when it was probably made entirely of wood, such a lamellaphone was a type widely distributed throughout the area. Its survival is probably due to the skill and ingenuity of the people who love to play this instrument. L. 17 cm (6¾ in.).

Appendices

Preceding double page:
A monk beating the gong at
the court of Louangphrabang
in Laos. Its reverberations
provide a solemn backdrop for
the unfolding of the ritual
ceremonies.

Acoustic nodes and antinodes: Acoustic nodes correspond to points at which the amplitude of air vibration is at a minimum, while antinodes correspond to points where it is at a maximum.

Aerophone: A musical instrument of the type in which the air itself forms the vibrator that causes sound to be produced. Ambient air may be in contact with the instrument (bull-roarers for example) or a vibrating air-column may be enclosed within the instrument (flutes, clarinets, horns etc.).

Autophone: see Idiophone.

Chordophone: A musical instrument having one or more strings held under tension and caused to vibrate by plucking, bowing, rubbing etc.

Diaphony: Term used in the Middle Ages to mean two-part polyphonic music.

Drone: The bass pipe of wind instruments such as bagpipes or pan-pipes; it has no lateral holes and therefore gives the same note continuously.

Frequency: The number of cycles of vibration per second, usually expressed in hertz (Hz), one hertz being one cycle per second. Frequency determines the pitch of sound.

Idiophone (from the Greek *idios* meaning 'own'): A musical instrument in which sound is produced by causing the (rigid) material of which it is made to vibrate. This vibration may be effected by percussion or concussion, plucking, rubbing, shaking etc.

Lamellaphone: A musical instrument of the idiophone family, consisting of a series of flexible tongues (made of metal or vegetable material) mounted on a board or on the wall of a soundbox. The musician plucks the projecting ends of the tongues. Examples are the African *sansa* and *mbira*.

Lithophone: A percussion instrument consisting of one or more slabs of stone.

Megaphone: A wide cylindrical tube (such as a thick piece of bamboo cane) or funnel-shaped device which concentrates the energy of the voice, projecting it in one direction.

Membranophone: A musical instrument which produces sound when one or more stretched membranes, usually of animal skin, are caused to vibrate.

Metallophone: A musical instrument incorporating metallic elements which are struck, as in the case of the xylophone, to produce a resonance.

Mode: Term used since the Early Middle Ages, which has come to have a whole range of different meanings. In the context of non-European music, 'modes' imply not so much scales as collections of motifs, phrases and formulas characteristic of a particular musical aesthetic.

Monody: Music consisting of only one melodic line, executed by an unaccompanied solo singer or by an instrument capable of emitting only one sound at a time.

Ostinato (Italian): Short melodic motifs, often in a low register, which are repeated many times without variation.

Polyphony: Term designating music in which two or more musical lines are played at the same time. Particular structural principles govern the association between the lines of music.

Polyrhythm: Simultaneous overlapping of two or more different rhythms in a musical texture consisting of several parts.

Rubato (Italian *tempo rubato* meaning 'robbed time'): Type of musical performance in which strict time is disregarded, and the rhythm of a melody is slightly distorted by holding back on certain notes and compensating for this on others.

Sympathetic strings: Additional metal strings stretched below the principal playing strings that are directly plucked or bowed by the musician. Sympathetic strings are activated by the vibration of the principal strings, and produce a low but continuous background resonance that enriches the timbre of instrumental sound.

Temperament: Term for the adjustment of intervals in a musical scale. Musical instruments in the Western classical tradition now use 'equal' temperament, in which the octave is divided into twelve equal semitones.

Timbre: The specific quality of a note, determined by the harmonics that accompany the fundamental tone. A particular timbre makes possible the recognition of the sound of a musical instrument and serves to distinguish the different ways in which it may be played.

Tonality: The organization of various pitches in a system which defines the relative importance of sounds as between themselves.

Tremolo (Italian 'trembling'): Confusion of terminology surrounds the terms 'tremolo' and 'vibrato'. 'Tremolo' is usually taken by musicologists to denote a change of intensity on one note.

Vibrato (Italian): Slight wavering of pitch to intensify the tone of a voice or instrument. Sometimes used to describe the repetition at regular intervals of one note (see Tremolo).

Collections of Musical Instruments

This selective list of major public collections of ethnic instruments includes for the most part those outside the countries or regions of origin and use. A comprehensive list of ethnographic collections, both public and private, including those in national museums, may be found in the *New Grove Dictionary of Music and Musicians*.

Austria
Museum für Völkerkunde, Vienna

Belgium
Etnografisch Museum, Antwerp

Canada
National Museum of Man, Ottawa
Ethnography Museum, University of British Columbia, Vancouver

Denmark
Nationalmuseet, Copenhagen

France
Musée de l'Homme, Paris

Germany
Museum für Völkerkunde, Berlin
Übersee-Museum, Bremen
Städtisches Museum für Völkerkunde, Frankfurt am Main

Great Britain
University Museum of Archaeology and Ethnology, Cambridge
British Museum, London
Horniman Museum, London
Pitt Rivers Museum, University of Oxford, Oxford

Hungary
Néprajzi Múzeum [Ethnographic Museum], Budapest

India
Indian Museum, Calcutta

Italy
Museo 'Luigi Pigorini', Rome
Pontifico Museo Missionario Etnologico, Vatican City

Netherlands
Tropen Museum, Amsterdam
Museum voor Land- en Volkenkunde, Rotterdam
Rijksmuseum voor Volkenkunde, Leiden

Norway
Etnografisk Museum, University of Oslo, Oslo

Poland
Pánstwowe Muzeum Etnograficzne [National Museum of Ethnology], Warsaw

Portugal
Museu Etnografico do Ultramar, Lisbon

Russia
Muzey Antropologii i Etnografii imeni Petra I, St Petersburg
State Historical Museum, Moscow

South Africa
South African Cultural History Museum, Cape Town
Africana Museum, Johannesburg

Sweden
Etnografiska Museet, Göteborg
Etnografiska Museet, Stockholm

Switzerland
Museum für Völkerkunde, Geneva
Schweizerisches Museum für Volkskunde, Basel
Musée d'Ethnographie de Neuchâtel, Neuchâtel

United States of America
Robert H. Lowie Museum of Anthropology, University of California, Berkeley (CA)
Museum of Fine Arts, Boston (MA)
Peabody Museum of Archaeology and Ethnology, Harvard University, Cambridge (MA)
World Music Collection, Wesleyan University, Middletown (CT)
Peabody Museum of Natural History, Department of Anthropology, Yale University, New Haven (CT)
American Museum of Natural History, New York (NY)
University of Pennsylvania Museum, Philadelphia (PA)
United States National Museum (Smithsonian Institution), Museum of Natural History, Washington, D.C.

Acknowledgments

The author is most grateful to Carole Daprey and the editorial team at Editions La Martinière for their constant support, and special thanks are due to Madeleine Leclair, whose skills have been of the greatest help.

The publishers wish to thank Marise Delaplanche, of the Musée de l'Homme, for her valuable assistance. The Chinese ideograms reproduced on pp. 101, 121 and 188 were drawn by Lucie Rault. Captions to the illustrations and the glossary entries were compiled by Madeleine Leclair.

Photographic illustrations, identified by page number(s), were supplied by the following:
6 (**above**): Stone/D. A. Brandt
6 (**below**): Rapho/Roland and Sabrina Michaud
7 (**above**): Hoa-Qui/M. Renaudeau
7 (**below**): N. Nilsson
8: RMN/Kodansha
10–11: Jacana/A. Shah
13: Jacana/Aberham
14: J. Vertut
15: Musée de l'Homme/D. Ponsard [M.H. 87.31.170]
16–17: Stone/A. & L. Sinibaldi
18–19: Explorer/M. Cambazard
20–21: Musée de l'Homme
22–23 (**left to right**): Explorer/M. Cambazard; Musée de l'Homme/Bader; Explorer/C. Michel; J. Vertut
24–25: Jacana/CPFB
26–27: Magnum/C. de Keyzer
28–29: Hoa-Qui/J.-D. Joubert
30: Cosmos/Maitre
31: Rapho/Roland and Sabrina Michaud
32: M. Guyot

33: Musée National de la Préhistoire, Les Eyzies; RMN/L. Hamon
34: Musée National de la Préhistoire, Les Eyzies
35: J. Villeminot
36 (**below left**): Musée de l'Homme/D. Ponsard [M.H. 93.1.77; M.H. 39.25.428; M.H. 87.101.700]
36–37 (**above centre**): Musée de l'Homme/D. Ponsard [M.H. 31.4.393]
36–37 (**below centre**): Musée de l'Homme/D. Ponsard [M.H. 28.27.31]
37 (**above**): Musée de l'Homme/D. Ponsard [M.H. 34.188.1425]
38 (**above**): G. Rouget
38 (**below**): Musée de l'Homme/D. Ponsard [M.H. 87.101.821]
39: G. Rouget
41: Musée d'Aquitaine, Bordeaux/J.-M. Arnaud
42–43: Hoa-Qui/M. Ascari
45: AKG photo
46–47: S. Chirol
48: Giraudon/Alinari
50–51: Magnum/Henri Cartier-Bresson
52: Magnum/Eve Arnold
53: Musée de l'Homme/D. Destable and J. Oster [M.H. 57.61.3–4]
54: Hoa-Qui/M. Huet
55: Hoa-Qui/L. & J. Lenars
56–57: Hoa-Qui/M. Renaudeau
59: © British Museum, London
60–61: Library of Congress, Washington, D.C.
62–63: Musée de l'Homme/J.-Y. Clavreul
64: N. Nilsson
65: M. Acconiato
66 (**above**): Musée de l'Homme/M. Delaplanche [M.H. 33.52.124]
66 (**below**): Musée de l'Homme/M. Delaplanche [M.H. 61.121.191]

67 (**above**): Musée de l'Homme/M. Delaplanche [M.H. 71.44.102]
68–69: Hoa-Qui/M. Renaudeau
70: Musée de l'Homme/Congo Presse/J. Mulders
71: Musée de l'Homme/M. Delaplanche [M.H. 31.74.299]
72–73: Hoa-Qui/Y. Gellie
74: Hoa-Qui/N. Thibaut
75: Musée de l'Homme/M. Delaplanche [M.H. 87.155.21]
76–77: Musée de l'Homme/Congo Presse
78: Stone/C. Jones
79: Hoa-Qui/M. Denis-Huot
80: Hoa-Qui/Y. Arthus-Bertrand
81: Hoa-Qui/de Wilde
82: Stone/M. Benson
83: Musée de l'Homme/D. Ponsard [M.H. 78.15.57(2)]
84: Giraudon
85: Centre Georges Pompidou/Musée National d'Art Moderne, Paris (© Man Ray Trust/ADAGP, Paris, 2000)
86 (**left**): RMN/Musée des Arts Africains et Océaniens/J.-G. Berizzi
86 (**right**): Musée de l'Homme/M. Delaplanche [M.H. 01.330.29]
87 (**left**): Musée de l'Homme/M. Delaplanche [M.H. 980.53.1]
87 (**right**): RMN/Chuzeville
88–89: Selva/Grafica
90: Rapho/Roland and Sabrina Michaud
91: Musée de l'Homme/M. Delaplanche [M.H. 976.107.1]
92–93: Selva/J.-C. See
95: Library of Congress, Washington, D.C.
96–97: Rapho/Roland and Sabrina Michaud
98–99: Giraudon/Lauros
100: Giraudon/Art Resource
102–103: Library of Congress, Washington, D.C.

104–105: RMN/Arnaudet
106: Musée de l'Homme/Tounanoff
107: Musée de l'Homme/M. Delaplanche [M.H. 82.66.1–2]
108: A. David-Neel
109: Image Bank/H. Sund
110: Rapho/Roland and Sabrina Michaud
111: Image Bank/H. Sund
112–113: RMN/G. Blot
114 (left): Musée de l'Homme/M. Delaplanche [M.H. 47.85.2]
114 (right): Musée de l'Homme/M. Delaplanche [M.H. 67.116.27]
115 (above): Musée de l'Homme/M. Delaplanche [M.H.970.51.181]
115 (below): Musée de l'Homme/M. Delaplanche [M.H. 986.21.1]
117: Artephot/J. Lavaud
118–119: Explorer/C. Boisvieux
120: RMN
122: Image Bank/ Meng Xiang Wang
123: Musée de l'Homme/M. Delaplanche [M.H. D-59.5.82]
124: RMN
125: Selva/J.-C. See
126: Corbis-Sygma/Keren Su
127: S. Held
128–129 (left to right): G. Rouget; Verger; G. Rouget
130 (above and left): Institut Européen d'Art Campanaire, Toulouse
131: Image Bank/H. Sund
132: VU/M. Ricard
133: ANA/J. Rey
134: RMN/R. Lambert
135: Hoa-Qui/M. Renaudeau
136–137: Stone/A. Cassidy
139: Stone/S. Weinberg
140–141: Stone/S. Huber
142: S. Held
143: Lucie Rault
144: Musée de l'Homme/M. Delaplanche [M.H. 67.111.429]
145: Marc Riboud
146–147: Magnum/Inge Morath
148: Giraudon
149: Musée Royal de l'Afrique Centrale, Tervuren/H. Lang

150–151: H. Zemp
152 (left): Giraudon
152–153: Rapho/Roland and Sabrina Michaud
154 (left): Musée de l'Homme/M. Delaplanche [M.H. 979.89.1]
155 (left): Musée de l'Homme/M. Delaplanche [M.H. 991.268.1]
155 (centre): Musée de l'Homme/M. Delaplanche [M.H. 997.30.1]
155 (right): Musée de l'Homme/M. Delaplanche [M.H. 47.70.1]
156: Scala, Florence
157: Stone/D. A. Brandt
158–159: Magnum/J. Koudelka
161: Giraudon, © ADAGP, Paris, 2000
162–163: VU/G. Iturbide
164: Hoa-Qui/Serena
165: Hoa-Qui/Rachoussof
166: Giraudon
167: Magnum/Werner Bischof
168: Giraudon
169: Giraudon
170–171: Staatliche Museen Preußischer Kulturbesitz, Berlin/M. Büsing
172: D.R./Documentation M. Helffer
173: Explorer/Bordes
174–175: H. Zemp
176: Musée de l'Homme/M. Delaplanche [M.H. 51.10.23]
177 (above): Musée de l'Homme/M. Delaplanche [M.H. x.org.4]
177 (centre): Musée de l'Homme/M. Delaplanche [M.H. x.org.5]
177 (below): Musée de l'Homme/M. Delaplanche [M.H. 39.105.2]
178–179: Explorer/D. Riffet
181: Rapho/Roland and Sabrina Michaud
182: Cosmos/Visions/A. Bradshaw
183: Côté Vues/C. Paul
184: H. Zemp
185: Musée de l'Homme/Gaillard
186: VU/M. Ricard
187: Musée de l'Homme/B. Hatala [M.H. D-33.6.4]
189: S. Held
190–191: Roger-Viollet

192: Lapad-Viollet
193: Stone/B. Forster
194: Gamma/M. Deville
195: Stone/D. Ash
196 (above): Musée de l'Homme/M. Delaplanche [M.H. 69.38.60]
196 (below): Musée de l'Homme/M. Delaplanche [M.H. 33.165.138]
197 (above): Musée de l'Homme/M. Delaplanche [M.H. 35.98.141]
197 (below): Musée de l'Homme/M. Delaplanche [M.H. 67.111.431]
198: Musée de l'Homme/Fedry
199: Côté Vues/W. Louvet
200 (left): Musée de l'Homme/M. Delaplanche [M.H. 55.78.3]
200 (right): Musée de l'Homme/M. Delaplanche [M.H. 991.268.1]
201 (above): Musée de l'Homme/M. Delaplanche [M.H. D-31.4.6]
201 (below): Musée de l'Homme/M. Delaplanche [M.H. 69.9.1; M.H. 8.24.189; M.H. 61.114.311; M.H. 93.1.77]
202: Musée de l'Homme/M. Delaplanche [M.H. 40.29.12]
203: Musée de l'Homme/J. Dournes
204–205: VU/M. Ricard
206: Côté Vues/Garp
207: Musée de l'Homme/M. Delaplanche [M.H. 71.44.98 and 71.44.358]
208: Hoa-Qui/M. Huet
209: G.Rouget
210: H. Zemp
211: Musée de l'Homme/M. Delaplanche [M.H. 45.17.171]
212–213: H. Zemp
214–215: H. Zemp
216: Musée de l'Homme/Verdier
217: Magnum/I. Berry
218 (left): Musée de l'Homme/M. Delaplanche [M.H. 970.31.2]
218 (right): Musée de l'Homme/M. Delaplanche [M.H. 61.120.100]
219 (above): Musée de l'Homme/M. Delaplanche [M.H. 980.111.4]
219 (below): Musée de l'Homme/M. Delaplanche [M.H. 67.87.52]
220–221: Hoa-Qui/J.-L. Dugast

Anoyanakis, Fivos, *Greek Popular Musical Instruments*, Athens, National Bank of Greece, 1979

Arnold, Denis (ed.), *The New Oxford Companion to Music*, Oxford, 1983

Aubert, Laurent, *Planète musicale, Catalogue du Musée d'Ethnographie de Genève*, Ivrea (TO), 1991

Baines, Anthony, *Musical Instruments through the Ages*, New York, Galpin Society, Walker, 1976 (first published 1961);

——, *The Oxford Companion to Musical Instruments*, Oxford and New York, 1992

Basset, Catherine, *Musiques de Bali à Java, l'ordre et la fête*, Paris and Arles, 1995 (including CD)

Bebey, Francis, *Musique de l'Afrique*, Paris, 1969

Bellow, A., *Illustrated History of the Guitar*, New York, 1970

Beurdeley, C. and Beurdeley, M., *Giuseppe Castiglione: A Jesuit Painter at the Court of the Chinese Emperors*, Rutland (Vermont), London and Tokyo, 1971

Blacking, John A.R., *How Musical is Man?*, Seattle (Washington), 1973

Blades, James, *Percussion Instruments and their History*, London, 1974 (first published 1970)

Brandily, Monique, *Instruments de musique et musiciens instrumentistes chez les Teda du Tibesti*, Tervuren, Annales du Musée Royal de l'Afrique Centrale, 1974;

——, *Introduction aux musiques africaines*, Paris and Arles, 1997 (including CD)

Bril, Jacques, *À cordes et à cris, Origine et Symbolisme des Instruments de musique*, Paris, 1980

Brincard, Marie-Thérèse, 'Sounding Forms', in *Sounding Forms: African Musical Instruments*, New York, 1989

Büchner, Alexander, *Musical Instruments through the Ages*, London, 1957

Carrington, John F., *Talking Drums of Africa*, London, 1949

Collaer, Paul, *Music of the Americas*, New York and Washington, 1973

Combarieu, Jules, *La Musique et la Magie, Étude sur les origines populaires de l'art musical; son influence et sa fonction dans les sociétés*, Paris, 1909

Coover, James, *Musical Instrument Collections, Catalogues and Cognate Literature*, Detroit (Michigan), 1981

Dampierre, Éric de, *Harpes zandé*, Paris, 1991;

——, (ed.), *Une Esthétique perdue*, Paris, 1995

Dauvois, Michel, 'Les témoins sonores paléolithiques', in *IVᵉ Rencontres internationales d'archéologie musicale de l'ICTM*, Paris, 1994, pp. 153–206

Dauvois, Michel, Boutillon, Xavier, Fabre, Benoît and Verge, Marc-Pierre, 'Son et musique au paléolithique', *Pour la science*, 253 (1998), Paris, pp. 52–8

Day, C.R., *The Music and Musical Instruments of Southern India and the Decan*, Delhi, 1974 (first published 1891)

Deva, B. Chaitanya, *Musical Instruments of India: Their History and Development*, New Delhi, 1987 (first published 1978)

Devale, Sue Carole, 'Musical Instruments and Ritual: a Systematic Approach', *Journal of the American Musical Instrument Society*, 14 (1988);

——, 'Organizing Organology', in *Selected Reports in Ethnomusicology*, vol. VIII: 'Issues in Organology', Los Angeles, 1990, pp. 1–34

Diagram Group, *Les Instruments de musique du monde entier. Encyclopédie illustrée*, Paris, 1978

Dieterlen, Germaine, 'L'Image du corps et les composantes de la personne chez les Dogon', in *La Notion de personne en Afrique Noire*, Paris, 1973

Dieterlen, Germaine and Liegers, Z., 'Les tengere, instruments de musique bozo', *Objets et Mondes, La Revue du Musée de l'Homme*, Paris, Muséum National d'Histoire Naturelle, vol. 7/3 (1967), pp. 185–216

Dournes, Jacques, 'La musique des Joraï', *Objets et Mondes, La Revue du Musée de l'Homme*, Paris, Muséum National d'Histoire Naturelle, vol. 5/4 (1965), pp. 211–44

Dournon, Geneviève, 'Organology', in *Ethnomusicology, an Introduction*, The New Grove Handbooks in Music, London, 1992, pp. 245–300

During, Jean, *Musiques d'Asie centrale, L'esprit d'une tradition*, Paris and Arles, 1998 (including CD)

Fages, G. and Mourer-Chauviré, C., 'La flûte en os d'oiseau de la grotte sépulcrale de Veyreau (Aveyron) et inventaire des flûtes préhistoriques d'Europe', *La Faune et l'Homme Préhistorique: Mémoires de la Société Préhistorique Française*, Paris, vol. XVI, 1983, pp. 95–103

Fischer, Hans, *Sound-Producing Instruments in Oceania* (translated from the German by Philip W. Holzknecht), Boroko, Institute of Papua New Guinea Studies, 1983

Goormaghtigh, Georges, *L'Art du Qin, Deux textes d'esthétique musicale chinoise*, Brussels, Institut Belge des Hautes Études Chinoises, 1990

Haefer, J. Richard, 'North American Indian Musical Instruments', *Journal of the American Musical Instruments Society*, 1 (1975)

Hamblin, Dora Jane, 'The luthier's art reigns once more in old Cremona', *Smithsonian*, October 1983, pp. 92–8

Helffer, Mireille, *Mchod-Rol, Les Instruments de la musique tibétaine*, Paris, 1994

Hood, Mantle, *The Ethnomusicologist*, Kent (Ohio), 1982 (first published 1971)

Hornbostel, Erich M. von and Sachs, Curt, 'Systematik der Musikinstrumente: ein Versuch', *Zeitschrift für Ethnologie*, XLVI (1914), Berlin, pp. 553–90; English translation by Anthony Baines and Klaus P. Wachsmann, 'Classification of Musical Instruments', *Galpin Society Journal*, 14 (1961)

Izikovitz, Karl Gustav, *Musical and Other Sound Instruments of the South American Indians: A Comparative Ethnographical Study*, Gothenburg, 1970 (first published 1934)

Jenkins, Jean and Rovsing-Olsen, P., *Music and Musical Instruments in the World of Islam*, London, 1976

Jouffray, Alain, *Art campanaire*, Toulouse, Centre-Musée Européen de l'Isle-Jourdain, 1993

Juzhong, Zang, Harbottle, Garman, Wang Changsui and Kong Zhoachen, 'Oldest playable musical instruments found at Jiahu early Neolithic site in China', *Nature*, London, 23 Sept. 1999, pp. 366–68

Kartomi, Margaret J., *Musical Instruments of Indonesia*, Melbourne, 1985;

——, *On Concepts and Classifications of Musical Instruments*, Chicago and London, 1990

Kirby, Percival R., *The Musical Instruments of the Native Races of South Africa*, London, 1934

Knudsen, E., 'Comment les chouettes localisent les sons', *Pour la science*, 52, Paris, 1982, pp. 32–45

Kothari, Komal S., *Indian Folk Musical Instruments*, New Delhi, 1968

Krishnaswami, S., *Musical Instruments of India*, Boston (Massachusetts), 1971

Kunst, Jaap, *Indonesian Music and Dance: Traditional Music and its Interaction with the West*, Amsterdam, Royal Institute, University of Amsterdam, 1994

Lagrange, Frédéric, *Musiques d'Égypte*, Paris, Cité de la musique / Arles, Actes Sud, coll. 'Musiques du monde', 1996 (including CD)

Le Gonidec, Marie-Barbara, Garcia, Léonardo and Caussé, René, 'Au sujet d'une flûte paléolithique, En souvenir de Dominique Buisson', *Antiquités Nationales*, 28, Paris, 1996, pp. 149–52

Leroi-Gourhan, André, *The Art of Prehistoric Man in Western Europe* (translated by Norbert Guterman), London, 1968

Lestrange, Marie-Thérèse de and Gessain, Monique, *Collections Bassari: Sénégal, Guinée*, Catalogues du Musée de l'Homme, Paris, Muséum National d'Histoire Naturelle, Série C–Afrique noire, 1976

Lindsay, Jennifer, *Javanese Gamelan*, Kuala Lumpur, 1979

Lortat-Jacob, Bernard, 'Jeu de métamorphoses: "launeddas" de Sardaigne', in *L'Improvisation dans les musiques de tradition orale*, Paris, 1987, pp. 255–66

Mahillon, Victor-Charles, *Catalogue descriptif et analytique du Musée instrumental du Conservatoire royal de musique de Bruxelles* (2nd ed.), Ghent, 1922 (reprinted 1978)

Maioli, Walter, *Son et Musique, leurs origines*, Paris, 1991

Malm, William P., *Japanese Music and Musical Instruments*, Rutland (Vermont) and Tokyo, 1959

Marcuse, Sibyl, *Musical Instruments. A Comprehensive Dictionary*, New York, 1964, and London, 1966

Michaud-Pradeilles, Catherine, *L'Organologie*, Paris, 1983

Montagu, Jeremy, *The World of Medieval and Renaissance Musical Instruments*, Newton Abbot, 1976

Montagu, Jeremy and Burton, John, 'A Proposed New Classification System for Musical Instruments', *Ethnomusicology*, 15/1 (1971), Champaign (Illinois), pp. 49–70

Montandon, Georges, *La généalogie des instruments de musique et les cycles de civilisation. Étude suivie du catalogue raisonné des instruments de musique du Musée ethnographique de Genève*, Geneva, Archives Suisses d'Anthropologie Générale, vol. 3/1, 1919

Moyle, Richard, *The Sounds of Oceania: An Illustrated Catalogue of the Sound-producing Instruments of Oceania in the Auckland Institute Museum*, Auckland, 1989

Muskett, Doreen, *Method for the Vielle or Hurdy-Gurdy*, London, 1982

Myers, Helen, 'African Music', 'American Indian Music', 'Pacific Islands', 'South-East Asian Music', in Denis Arnold (ed.), *The New Oxford Companion to Music*, Oxford, 1983

Nettl, Bruno, *The Study of Ethnomusicology, Twenty-nine Issues and Concepts*, Urbana (Illinois), 1983

Norborg, Ake, *A Handbook of Musical and Other Sound-producing Instruments from Equatorial Guinea and Gabon*, Stockholm, Musikmuseets Skrifter 16, 1989

Olsen, Dale, 'The Ethnomusicology of Archeology: A Model for the Musical /

Cultural Study of Ancient Material Culture', in *Selected Reports in Ethnomusicology*, vol. VIII: 'Issues in Organology', Los Angeles, 1990, pp. 175–97

Ortiz, Fernando, *Los Instrumentos de la musica afro-cubana*, 4 vols., Havana, 1952–55

Otte, Marcel (ed.), *Sons originels, Préhistoire de la musique*, in *Actes du colloque de musicologie (décembre 1992)*, Liège, ERAUL 61, 1994

Picken, Laurence, *Folk Musical Instruments of Turkey*, London, 1975

Price, Percival, *Bells and Man*, Oxford, 1983

Qassim Hassan, Sheherazade, *Les Instruments de musique en Irak et leur rôle dans la société traditionnelle*, Paris / The Hague, 1980

Rault, Lucie, 'Autour du zheng, Un essai de filiation de quelques cithares d'Asie orientale', in *Cahiers de musiques traditionnelles*, vol. 2: 'Instrumental', Geneva, 1989, pp. 63–74;

——, *La Cithare chinoise* zheng, *un vol d'oies sauvages sur les cordes de soie...*, Paris, 1987;

——, 'L'harmonie du centre, aspects rituels dans la Chine Ancienne', in *Cahiers de Musiques traditionnelles*, vol. V: 'Musiques rituelles', Geneva, 1992, pp. 111–25;

——, 'L'homme musical', in *Trésors méconnus du Musée de l'Homme*, Paris, 1999;

——, 'Villoteau et la musique égyptienne, ou l'éveil à la musique de l'Autre', in *L'Expédition d'Égypte, une entreprise des Lumières 1798–1801*, Paris, Académie des Sciences, 1999, pp. 217–28

Remnant, Mary, *Musical Instruments. An Illustrated History from Prehistory to the Present*, London, 1989

Reznikoff, Iégor, 'Sur la dimension sonore des grottes à peintures du paléolithique', in *Comptes rendus de l'Académie des sciences*, Paris, vol. 304, série II, 1987, pp. 153–56; vol. 305, série II, 1987, pp. 307–10

Reznikoff, Iégor and Dauvois, Michel, 'Sur la dimension sonore des grottes ornées', *Bulletin de la Société préhistorique française*, vol. 8515 (1988), pp. 238–46

Rimmer, *Ancient Musical Instruments of Western Asia in the British Museum*, London, 1969

Rouget, Gilbert, *La Musique et la Transe, Esquisse d'une théorie générale des relations de la musique et de la possession*, Paris, 1990 (first published 1981);

——, *Un roi africain et sa musique de cour, Chants et danses au palais à Porto-Novo sous le règne de Gbèfa (1948–1976)*, Paris, 1996 (including 2 CDs and video cassette)

Rovsing-Olsen, Miriam, *Chants et Danses de l'Atlas (Maroc)*, Paris and Arles, 1997 (including CD)

Sachs, Curt, *Handbuch der Musikinstrumentenkunde*, Leipzig, 1920;

——, *The History of Musical Instruments*, New York, 1940

Sadie, Stanley (ed.), *New Grove Dictionary of Musical Instruments* (3 vols.), London, 1984

Santiago, Chiori, 'Carillons: making heavy-metal music with staying power', *Smithsonian*, November 1994, pp. 113–25

Schaeffner, André, *Origine des instruments de musique, Introduction ethnologique à l'histoire de la musique instrumentale*, Paris / The Hague, 1994 (first published 1968)

Schneider, Marius, 'Primitive music', in *New Oxford History of Music*, vol. 1: *Ancient and Oriental Music*, London, 1975, pp. 1–82

Scothern, Paula M.T., 'Paleo-organology, Ethnomusicology and the Historical Dimension', in *Ethnomusicology and the Historical Dimension*, London, 1986, pp. 19–24

Speranza, Gaëtano, 'Sculpter au singulier' and 'Sculpture sans sculpteur?', in Dampierre, Éric de, *Une esthétique perdue*, Paris, 1995, pp. 21–53 and 77–87

Stevenson, Robert, *Music in Aztec and Inca Territory*, Los Angeles, 1968

Tranchefort, François-René, *Les Instruments de musique dans le monde*, 2 vols., Paris, 1980

Trân Quang Haï, Asselineau, Michel and Bérel, Eugène, *Musiques du monde* (teaching manual, including 3 CDs), Courlay, 1993

Trân Van Khê, *Musique du Viet-Nam*, Paris, 1996 (first published 1967)

Vandor, Ivan, *La Musique du Bouddhisme tibétain*, Paris, 1976

Villoteau, Guillaume-André, *Description historique, technique et littéraire des Instruments de musique des Orientaux*, Paris, 1813;

——, *Mémoire sur la musique de l'antique Égypte*, Paris, 1816

Wegner, Ulrich, *Afrikanische Saiteninstrumente*, Berlin, Museum für Völkerkunde, 1984

Zemp, Hugo, *Musique dan, La musique dans la pensée et la vie sociale d'une société africaine*, Paris / The Hague, 1971;

——, 'Fabrication des flûtes de Pan aux îles Salomon', *Objets et Mondes, La Revue du Musée de l'Homme*, 12/3 (1972), Paris, Muséum National d'Histoire Naturelle, pp. 247–68;

——, 'Melanesian Solo Polyphonic Panpipe Music', *Ethnomusicology* 25, no. 3 (1981)

Index of Instruments and Types

Page numbers in italics refer to captions to the illustrations.